W9-CFX-565

ADD ONE COSSACK
AND STIR . . .

John John Dyck
1961

ADD ONE COSSACK

AND STIR...

The Life Story Of John John Dyck

As Told To
Sylvia Murray Dyck

DORRANCE & COMPANY
Philadelphia

Just as it is the obligation of a good farmer to rebuild and revitalize the soil which has given him life and sustenance, so is it also his duty to teach those who will follow him to love their soil and respect its riches.

Mr. Dyck has left the record of his life both as a heritage for his children and grandchildren and as a "thank you" to two countries which gave him safety, opportunity and freedom.

It is offered to you, the reader, in the hope that you will hold your lands and freedoms as a sacred trust.

CONTENTS

ILLUSTRATIONS

MAPS AND CHARTS

FOREWORD

Some parts of this narrative may be vague, as the incidents recorded herein were written many years after they were experienced. The stories were very vivid, however, to the teller.

Participating in killing and other brutalities of war during the Russian Revolution created conflicts in the conscience of this gentle, peace-oriented person.

The mind is a vast storehouse of old etchings, with impressions made on the mind borne for a lifetime. A man in wakefulness is able to control his memory with deplorable experiences erased. Within the subconsciousness of rest, however, sleep robs man of his guard and opens Pandora's box to allow ghosts from the past to escape upon the slightest provocation.

Mr. Dyck had been plagued by nightmares since his youth. In searching his memory to record the story of his life, the memory cells of his mind were reactivated and events of his war time experiences began to frequent him more often in dreams. In an effort to avoid further distress of this nature, the narrative about the Revolution was discontinued leaving much of what he saw and experienced unwritten.

—S.M.D.

A GLIMPSE OF THE MAN

"Where have you been? Didn't you get any Russian history or geography in school?"

When put on the spot with questions like these, I began to wonder why I knew so little about some things. Some information must have been presented at school, but the exposure failed to inspire me to further inquiry. Russian names were too long, and the places—impossible to pronounce. It looked like a pretty difficult and involved subject. Being averse to intellectual study, I managed to skip this area, along with others, and focused my youthful attention on things important to me at the time. Early adulthood offered more exposure, but by now I had become an apt student in the art of half-hearing, half-reading and half-seeing.

Thus I came to hear the following adventures unprepared and unable to fake intellect. With this open truth, I was able to say, "Just tell me about it. I'll ask you questions. Don't assume that I know anything."

On this basis we went to work. He could speak seven languages and write four. He said English was the hardest for him; his writing confused me. No matter how many pages he wrote, it was all one continuous paragraph. On the third page, in the same paragraph, he would explain something he had said on the first page. On page twenty, he might easily throw in a little more about what he had written the week before.

We made great sport of our spelling. I corrected him on scool (school) and wat (what)—understandable mistakes for him, and he found some of my inexcusable ones. Through it all we laughed and talked and talked and wrote, and as we worked a mutual bond and admiration grew between us.

I teased him about the things he didn't tell, especially his love life. I would say, "Tell about the haystacks." He would just laugh. John said that he would not tell of the people he had killed and the bad things he had done. I could reassure him here. Anyone would realize that a soldier, enduring a revolution, could not long exist in sainthood.

There he sat, across from me at the table, telling story after story in his heavy accent. Some of the accounts were hair-raising. Some were simple tales. The listener could not help cocking one ear and studying the man to ascertain whether or not he was "putting you on."

He certainly seemed sincere enough. Looking at him, you weren't quite sure, however, as he smiled a broad smile and looked into your eyes while he talked. His face was impossible to read. It was either the true poker face or the broad grinning face. I finally knew that he was watching me for signs of understanding and belief.

If someone told you about beans which were so long that they were carried over the shoulder and touched the ground on either side, would you believe him? I was always asking, "Are you kidding?" He would blush, laugh and say, "No." Again I wouldn't know for sure.

A good storyteller does things with his voice to create atmosphere, mood, and emotion for his listeners. What would "I-want-my-gol-den arm" be as a spooky story, without a mysterious voice?

John Dyck failed the voice test. He didn't want to shock or scare his listeners. He just wanted to tell about the things that happened. He made an effort to soft pedal his stories. He especially wanted his children to know how lucky they were to live where they were free. He could do this best with accounts of his past life, and he chose to do it without startling terms. He would relate that the soldiers had "sax" with the women—and be halfway into another story before I would realize that he meant "The soldiers raped the women." This certainly changed his meaning.

His hair was snow-white and he patted a slightly rounded stomach. His appearance was of a strong healthy man in his middle fifties, though his years numbered sixty-four. He was not tall, standing five feet, eight inches, and not handsome. His nose was too large and it hooked. He referred to his nose laughingly, wondering why Durante had become so famous instead of him, when his nose could easily compete.

I had known since I was a child that Mr. Dyck was a Russian and that the family was Dutch. What I didn't realize was that he considered himself to be a Dutchman born in Russia—NOT the same at all.

Though he was a man in every sense, John did not consider helping around the house "sissy." He was as likely to be found washing dishes and cooking as fixing an electrical appliance or tearing an automobile apart. He was talented with his hands and seemed to be able to do anything. He liked keeping busy and being helpful.

He was never without a story or an adventure. A short walk around the block brought him back full of information. He would be holding a plant, some rock or some soil. He would have met someone with whom he had exchanged stories. He made you wonder if it were really your block that he had walked because he had observed it much more closely than you had ever seen it.

I found Mr. Dyck to be a sort of "black sheep" Mennonite—having long ago given up what I consider the narrow, restrictive code of some sects of that religion. He did not worry about my immortal soul being rejected because I found dancing a great joy or because I derived pleasure from occasional card playing. He did not frown on lipstick and jewelry and was not concerned with dress style. Being brought up in the Mennonite religion, without a doubt, had a bearing on the character of the man, however.

Although no group of people can be stereotyped, I have formed in my mind some generalities about the Mennonite people of my acquaintance. Generally these folk are a quiet, industrious people who do not glorify themselves or material possessions. They are concerned about the welfare of others.* They are a non-aggressive people, willing to turn the

---

* A recent example of the Mennonite way was shown nationally on television following the disruptive 1971 Mayday anti-war demonstrations in Washington, D.C. A Mennonite group arrived in West Potomac Park near the Jefferson Memorial where many of the Mayday coalitionists had camped. Without fanfare, they went to work picking up trash, rebuilding park benches and repairing the damage left by the previous group. While sharing anti-war feelings, the interest of this group was not in destroying but rebuilding.

other cheek. They do not expect life without tribulation. They acknowledge God as a personal friend and call on Him for strength—not miracles.

The reader must understand these things. He must not expect to find in these pages a magnificent story of the big "I" but should instead be prepared only to share some experiences from the life of a common human being. No apology is offered for the lack of precise grammar in this account. Mr. Dyck was multilingual, but lacked a complete grasp of the English language. To completely rewrite his words would detract from the flavor of the truth in his story.

Armed with a vast background of experiences and an unquenchable thirst for knowledge, J.J.D. met each day with joy and was prepared to give and receive in the fascinating game of life. This narrative of one immigrant, known to only a few of us, is but one of the numerous stories brought to this western continent and lost in our vast melting pot.

S. M. D.

ACKNOWLEDGMENTS

I hereby gratefully express my appreciation and thanks to the following people who so willingly contributed both information and encouragement in order that this book could reach completion:

Dorothy Dyck, for documentation; the Dyck children, for wishing the book; Abram Dyck, for family data and map clarification; Agatha Dyck Langemann, for her account of the family; Essie Mellinger Schloneger, for information and research; the Mennonite Encyclopedia, Goshen College, Goshen, Indiana, for research; Walter Siegl, for the drawings; Walter and Renata Siegl, for translation; my family, for endurance, and nameless friends, for enthusiasm.

—S.M.D.

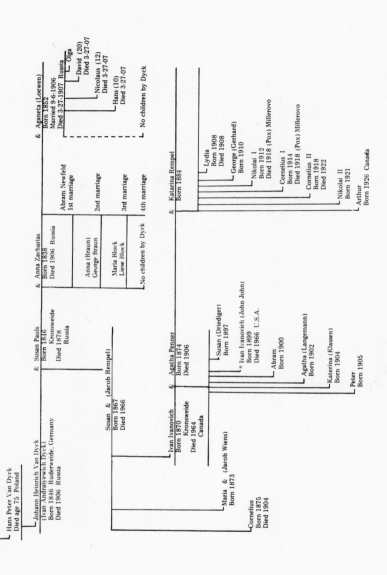

Chapter I

FAMILY BACKGROUND

My family name has changed through the years according to the country in which my people were living. In Holland, Van means "son of." My great-grandfather, born in Holland, was Hans Peter "son of" Dyck, thus Van Dyck.

The Van followed the family as it moved through Pomerania (northeast Germany) but there the first name, Hans, became Johann. In Russia, Johann changed again and became Ivan. In America, it became John.

In Russian, there is no notation such as the English "junior." In order to show family membership, middle names designate the father's first name. My father's name was Ivan Ivanovich Dyck (the letter "i" is pronounced as "e"). My brother's name was Abram Ivanovich Dyck. Wives' and daughters' middle names are also the father's first name. For example, my stepmother's name was Katarina Ivanovna ("na" is feminine) Dyck, and my sister's name was Susanna Ivanovna Dyck.

It has been traditional in my family to name the first son of the first son John, according to the nation's spelling. Considering the number of Johns in my background, it might have been wise for me to have broken the tradition but I did not. My first son carries my name and we continually receive the other's mail.

My papers, on examination, add to the confusion of names. My *Declaration of Alien About to Depart for the United States* named me Jean Yanovitch Dick, and the *Bureau Interallie de Controle des Passeports* called me Mr. Jean Ivanovileh Dick. The doctor who gave me my *Certificate of Health* in Constantinople, certified that he had examined Mr. Dick Yohann. The *Bureau Russe des Passeports*, Constantinople, gave Corporal Dick, Jean, authoriza-

1

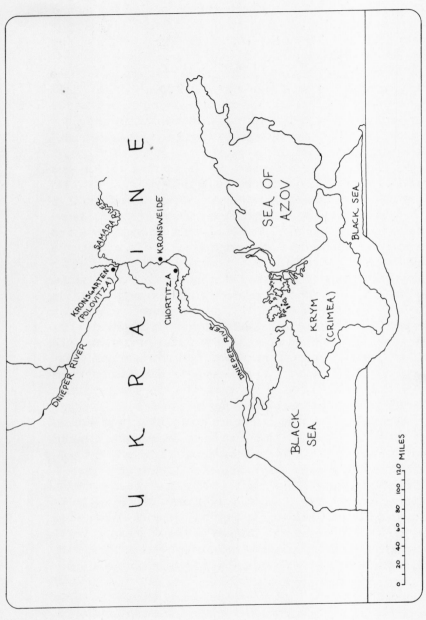

Settlement Area

2

tion to receive a normal passport, and that was what I wanted at the moment, so I didn't argue with anyone. I'll tell you about that later. I arrived in America being John Dick. You may call me John.

Two things can happen to a person who begins to trace and record his family. Either you yell, "Ach, #%*%@!" and throw away all those little note scraps or you get totally involved trying to track down correct information. Once involved, my family wouldn't let me stop. It was as though I were being carried along on a wave.

My family tree alone makes the population explosion a reality. The men of my family are long-lived and have made every effort to see that our family did not become extinct.

I discovered, in backtracking, that my great-great-grandfather, Hans Isaak Van Dyck, was born in the town of Workum, Holland. He was the mayor of Workum and died there at the age of sixty-two.

My great-grandfather, Hans Peter Van Dyck, was a teacher. He left Workum when he joined a group leaving Holland in the early 1800s because of religious persecution. The Dutch migrations of this period were in groups of hundreds. This Mennonite group migrated south into Luxemburg where they split into two groups. One went south into Switzerland, while my great-grandparents' group proceeded east through Germany to the province of Pomerania. This group was destined to enter Russia many years later.

Johann Heinrich Van Dyck, my grandfather, was born in Rudnerweide, Germany in 1846. When the migration moved again, it went through Poland to the border of Russia. Great-Grandfather died there at the age of seventy-five.

With the migration Great-Grandmother with her son, Johann, crossed the Russian border and settled close to Chortitza, in the Ukraine. The group numbered 288 families and was the first Mennonite settlement in Russia. Upon entering the country Grandfather's name was changed into Russian and recorded as Ivan Andraiyevich Dyck.

Another Dutch group came out of Prussia a few years later. Among this second group was Susan Pauls, who was to become grandfather's first wife. Both of these groups met at

Chortitza, which is at the bend of the Dnieper (Dnepr) River. These families settled seven colonies within a radius of about fifty miles.

Grandfather Ivan, who was a farmer, added only four children to these colonies himself, but was father to eight additional children of his second and third wives. (It should be pointed out to our modern generation that additional wives were not acquired as a result of divorce, but resulted after the death of each preceding wife.)

My father, Ivan Ivanovich, was born in Kronsgarten, the German name used in this narrative (Polovitza in Russian)* in 1870. Being the first son of the first son he was endowed with the traditional "John" name.

The Russian Ukraine, which is called the "breadbasket of Europe," was at that time open to settlers for the claiming of the land. The settlements can be compared to those made under the American land grants. The continuous overflowing of the Dnieper River which has deposited loam over some of the land for centuries, guaranteed this to be an ideal location for the Dutch farmer.

To give you an idea of the abundance of this land, I will mention the pumpkins which we raised in Kronsgarten. The wagons were not very big compared to American wagons, but it took three men to roll a pumpkin on a wagon. Three pumpkins made a load. Uncle Jacob Wiens had five acres of pumpkins. I recall a time when my cousin Jake Wiens and I went along to help get a load. We decided to try to walk across the field, walking on pumpkins. We did this and did not have to step on the ground at any time.

Much later, when I was still a newcomer in the United States, I was asked to speak to a young people's group at church about my early life in Russia. When I told this group

*The Russian alphabet has some single letters, with no English counterparts, which represent an accumulation of sounds. The Russian alphabet was changed after the Revolution, eliminating and changing many of their previously used letters. In translating Russian village names and proper names into English, I have attempted to spell it as it sounds. For the sake of consistency when variations in spelling have been found, I have chosen to use "v" instead of "w."

my "pumpkin story" they laughed. They thought I was joking. I tried to convince them that I was not, but I couldn't. I decided then that I would not make public speeches because I would not be believed.

I am telling you this to help you understand the reason for such quick prosperity in a new land. The Dutch settlements in Russia were affluent enough to send both students and missionaries to other countries and when the migration, which had gone to Switzerland, wanted to move on to America, the Russian Mennonites were able to help finance their move. In Kansas, Oklahoma, and Iowa today many Dutch names can be found. Many of these folk are descendants of the Swiss group. Many speak the Dutch dialect even after all these years.

Chapter II

THE SETTLEMENT

When the Mennonites first came to Russia, under Catherine the Great, they had to sign papers promising that they would not do any missionary work in Russia. Catherine said she needed soldiers, not ministers. Mennonites could send missionaries abroad, but could do no work at home. The church, therefore, was split and organized as a Mennonite Brethren Church in order to do missionary work where we lived.

Only Dutch people were allowed to live in the Dutch settlements. The *gendarme* and the herdsman with their families were the only exceptions. It was considered a privilege for these people to be able to live among the Dutch, as they were treated well. Their dwellings, which were built on the outskirts of the settlements, were usually six-room brick buildings. In the Russian peasant village their homes would probably be adobe. The children of these employees attended our schools.

The *gendarme* received his job as a reward. He was usually a retired army man who had served long and well in the tzar's army. He handled the small matters of law enforcement which occurred in the settlement. For those things which required court attention we had to go to the Russian courts in the city.

You may be wondering about the education in the settlements. The Dutch maintained their own schools. These were better than the Russian schools because of the quality of teachers and the number of subjects. In order to assure good teachers, the most brilliant students were selected and sponsored while they acquired their higher educations abroad. Students were sent to Germany, Switzerland, and Austria. In this way the Mennonites, through the years, built up excel-

6

lent high schools and colleges.

In grade schools boys and girls were mixed, but in high schools and colleges, boys and girls attended separate schools. In Chortitza, the girls' college had a seven-foot wall around it; the boys' college had a five-foot wall. Only men teachers were allowed in the boys' schools and only women teachers, with the exception of the principal, in the girls' school.

The principals were held responsible for the morals of the students. Schools and their administrators were governed by the Mennonite Boards of Education in the settlements. Students respected the teachers and were expected to tip their caps if they met a teacher on the street or anywhere else.

School children all wore uniforms. The girls wore a light-colored uniform dress with blue stripes running up and down. The boys wore dark gray. Our uniform jacket was similar to that worn by aviators minus the breast and side pockets. It had brass buttons in front and was accompanied by a high collar such as that worn by some ministers. We had a belt with a brass buckle, two inches by two inches, with the initials of the school in the center. Our visor cap also had a button in front with the school initial on it.

In order to have their own schools, the Dutch had to assure the Russian government that the Russian language would be taught. The Dutch language had not yet been written when grandfather was a child,* yet Dutch was the language spoken in our homes.

The main occupation of the Dutch people, at the beginning of the settlement period, was farming. The Dutch engaged in mixed farming by raising both crops and livestock. Grain is the crop most often thought of when the Ukraine is mentioned. Animals raised were dairy cattle, chickens, pigs and geese, to name a few. The Dutch used chaff to feed the stock, but because separators were not very good, in the days of my growing up, a lot of grain got into the chaff. Chaff and sliced pumpkins or beets were fed to the

---

* Mr. Dyck believed this, because all written and printed material he saw in his youth was in German. It was a common saying among Mennonites that God understood only German.

7

milk cows. The farms were equal to about fifty to sixty American acres.

Later, when the settlements were well established, people entered into other business occupations. My dad is an example of someone who entered another business. He owned a windmill in Kronsgarten which ground flour with stones—stone ground flour.

When the people of the settlement wanted to buy something, they had to go to nearby towns. I never saw a grocery or any other store owned by a Dutchman. The settlement people traded their surplus items in nearby towns.

Settlers were close-knit in their civic matters. In many respects life in the Dutch settlements in Russia resembled that of the American Mennonite in social life and custom.

The government of the village settlement was headed by a mayor, who was elected for a three-year term. He mediated with the government. Serving under him were the elders. There were usually fifteen elders in the larger villages; for smaller villages there were fewer elders.

When the village population became too large for the amount of land owned, the elders came together. They bought a big parcel of land, and created another settlement wherever they could buy big enough parcels. A school was always built for the new settlement; most Dutch buildings were made of brick.

A few years before World War I people started to branch out into different businesses. It was then to our advantage to have a representative in the Russian Duma (House of Representatives). Mr. Warkentine was elected by all the Dutch settlers to be the first representative to the Russian Duma.

I recall this story about Mr. Warkentine, a very obese person. For a long time, whenever the Duma was in session, he would fall asleep. When the session would be over and he would come home, the elders would ask him what had happened or why the Duma had done something. He would never know. The Dutch newspaper *Deutsche Nachricht* wrote an article saying that Mr. Warkentine was often asleep. Warkentine was very mad and told the newspaper to retract their statement. The next week the paper's headline read,

"Warkentine Wakes Up."

In the Dutch settlement, we did not have much in the way of recreation as you know it. The strictness of our religion forbade card playing or dancing. We had hayrides and, in the winter, sleigh rides. When the rivers were frozen, skating was the way of life.

The most common entertainment was a gathering of the young people in someone's home for games. This was the way young people got acquainted and eventually paired off for marriage.

My father married a settlement girl, Agatha Penner, in 1896. Aside from being a mill owner, Dad was a preacher in the Mennonite Brethren Church. Churches had two or three ministers, one a head minister and the others "fill in" or lay ministers. My father was a "fill in" minister.

In the settlement and in our homes, the church was the center of our life. We were guided by the Bible and its teachings. In our family Bible the following messages (paraphrased by translation) were left for us by my great-grandfather:

> Here I am giving you a book wherein you will find comfort and peace. Search and you shall find. "Delight thyself also in the Lord. He will give thee the desires of thine heart." Psalms 37:4. From what I have read in this book, I have gained exceedingly in spirit and courage. . . . In fields no little flowers bloom— what to do? Bloom in your heart. The memory is evergreen. Always go in clear pleasure with an upward look and through the dark valley without fear and cringing. Have the open heavens over you.
>
> "The Lord is near those of broken hearts. Many are the afflictions of the righteous, but the Lord delivereth him out of them all." Psalms 34:18-19. We enter into the kingdom of God through much tribulation. Through denials you must go if you want to see God's kingdom. . . . Trust in God's faithfulness. He will never betray you.
>
> "May the Lord our God be friendly toward us and bless the works of our hands. Yes the work of our hands he will demand." Psalms 90:17 . . . Let us strive for peace and love toward our fellow men be they German, Russian or Jew. We all have the same God and are all God's children. Among you let there be peace and love unto the grave. . . . Don't bicker and fight among yourselves . . .

Thus were we guided by our forefather. Often these teachings were needed for strength in troubled times.

9

Chapter III

EARLY CHILDHOOD

My parents gave to the world three sons and three daughters. Being the first son, I became Ivan Ivanovich, along with my dad.

I was born, August 10, 1899, in the settlement of Kronsgarten and spent my preschool years there. It is difficult to remember things that happened when I was very young. It seems strange that I best remember things learned from being on the wrong end of a stick.

I remember our first home and one frustrating incident that happened to me when I was a small boy. Dad's mill was on a hill across a valley from our house. Dad had made a round, red sign and mounted it on a handle. When dinner was ready, the sign was put through metal loops on the gate post. Dad could see the sign from the mill and would come home.

One day my mother asked me whether or not I thought I was big enough to put up the sign. "Sure I am," I said. I climbed the gate and tried to put the sign in the loops, but the wind was so strong that it knocked me off the gate. I tried many times in vain. It was very important to me that I succeed because Dad wouldn't get any dinner if he didn't see the signal. I had been given a mission which I could not accomplish. It did not occur to me that my mother could still hang the sign. My father was saved when a man came down the road and helped me.

That fall, I was allowed to go along in the wagons when Granddad sent three men and about eight peasant girls out along the river to pick corn. During the morning one of the girls was missing. I went to look for her in the corn rows. I found her having a baby. I stood and watched. She was crying and having a hard time. I sat on my haunches and waited until I saw the head come and then the baby. It was

10

illegitimate; the girl was soon back in the field picking corn.

Our family moved to the Russian village of Spaskoya when I was about five years old. My father built a mill there, run by steam engines. This village was about fifteen miles south of Kronsgarten. My playmates were Russian peasant children who spoke a Ukrainian dialect. In order to play with them I had to learn their language.

Our house in Spaskoya was new and needed painting. Mom was painting the steps leading to the attic. I wanted to help, naturally. Mom told me several times to go and play but like any child, I wanted to paint. I tormented and played around until I managed to upset all the paint. Mom was so mad that she took her slippers off and gave me a good shellacking. Little more than my feelings were hurt, but I learned my lesson through the seat of my pants.

I used to run all over the mill in Spaskoya. There were many dangerous places there with each drawing me like a magnet. One day I was walking past a machine that sifted the flour. At one end, the machinery had cogwheels and a belt to run it. There was a sharp wind coming through the window and it blew my shirt, which I wore out of my pants, into the cogs. The cogs started to creep up toward my neck. I was really scared. In trying to save myself, I got my hand twisted in the shirt too. With my shirt tail in a bundle and my hand and collar being pulled, the wind was squeezed out of me. At that point, the belt came off the machine and everything stopped.

The head miller came to see why the machine had stopped and found me in my predicament. He called my dad and Dad started to turn the wheel back. When I began to get some air, I started to cry at the top of my tonsils. I was more frightened than hurt.

When I was free Dad gave me a whaling. I think the accident badly frightened him. The spanking was his first reaction. To me though, it was adding insult to injury. I had been licked before and would be licked again, but this spanking really impressed me.

Because my parents wanted us to attend the Dutch school, and because there were none in Spaskoya, we children were destined to return to Kronsgarten to begin our schooling. It was necessary for us to board with relatives in order to do this.

My sister Susan had already been in school for one year; it was now my turn to go away to stay, and to begin school. No one mentioned the arrangements to me.

One Saturday, my father hitched up his pair of black stallions, of which he was very proud, and drove the family to Kronsgarten. We arrived the same day and stayed overnight at the home of my aunt, Susan Rempel. The next afternoon, everyone urged me to go over the hill to the woods to play. My family wanted to leave for home without my knowledge and they wanted me out of the way.

I was just about to start the descent down the far side of the hill when I looked back and saw the family leaving. I couldn't imagine why they would be leaving me. I ran to catch them, with everybody trying to catch me as I tore through the village in hot pursuit. My Aunt Susan lived at one end of the village, and my Aunt Maria and Uncle Jacob Wiens (with whom I was to stay that year) lived at the other. Uncle Jacob saw me coming and caught me. I was determined to pursue my family, but he was more determined that I should not. He happened to have a bridle in his hands and he gave me a beating with it. It was a good beating, and I was clearly impressed with his ability to cope with me. The next day I started to school.

Late in this school year, 1906, my dear mother passed away. My father married Katarina Rempel the next year and their union gave me six half brothers and one little sister. My half sister died in her first year. The results of my father's two marriages were thirteen children with nine surviving to adulthood.

In my first year and through each succeeding year, I was schooled in two languages. One was Russian because, as I have mentioned, the education department under the tzar required the Dutch to teach the Russian language in their schools. The other language was German. Our forefathers said that the good Lord understood only in German because Bibles were all printed in that language. We must, therefore, learn to read and speak in God's language.

When I was in my second year at school, my grandfather, Johann Heinrich Dyck, married for the third time. My new grandmother, Aganeta, had four children by a previous marriage. They lived in the house of my birth in Kronsgarten. Grandfather died two months and one day after their marriage.

One day, about five months after Grandfather's death, my new grandmother's sons Nicolaus, who was twelve years old and Hans, who was ten, did not come to school. Olga was out of the village visiting relatives and David, who was twenty, was working at home.

My teacher sent me to their family home to see why they were absent. When I got there, I saw that the front door was open so I went in. I found my grandmother lying on the floor in the living room. A crowbar had been driven through her ear and into the floor.

Terrified, I ran as fast as I could to tell my teacher. I ran past my Aunt Maria's nearby home and past many other homes without thinking of stopping. The school was in the middle of the village. The teacher sent all the children home and returned with me to my grandfather's home. Soon the entire village of eighteen families came to find out what had happened. We knew that Grandmother's eldest child, Olga, was gone. The boys, however, were not visible anywhere so we began searching for them.

We found Hans first. He was under his messed-up bed. His ears and nose had been cut off and the palms of his hands were all sliced. He had apparently wrapped himself in his sheets trying to alleviate his pain. He still moved a little when we found him, but soon died. David was found in the barn covered with chaff. Nicolaus had apparently been caught as he tried to flee from the barn. He was at a little door which led outside. Both boys had been beaten to death.

Because my grandfather had been a wealthy man, it was not hard to determine that robbery had motivated the murders. It was speculated that the robbers were recognized by their victims and were thus silenced.

My dad and his sisters offered fifty rubles (the equivalent

13

of fifty dollars) reward for information regarding the killers. This was a handsome offering at that time since a peasant could build an adobe home for that amount.

Two days later, a woman noticed tracks into a wheat field. This was near the Russian peasant village of Podgorodneye, which was ten miles from Kronsgarten. The two robbers were caught. They had been hiding in the field and had made tracks as they went in and out of hiding to get food.

These men had some of my grandparents' possessions with them, which proved their guilt. One robber, who had a badly mangled hand, was one of my father's machinists in the mill. He probably assumed that Grandfather had kept all of his money in the house, and had taken a buddy with him to get it. They had found about 1500 rubles, but had failed to find the secret compartment in grandfather's roll-up desk where most of the money in the house was kept. The greatest part of Grandfather's wealth was in the bank.

A Russian peasant mob wrote the finish to this story. The murderers were hung by their hands and feet and suspended under a bridge by a rope. A second rope was tied to their waists and used to swing them like a pendulum, bumping their heads and rears against either side of the rock embankments of the bridge. This continued for four or five hours until they were dead.

During my grade school years, I had my room and board with my aunts; one year with Aunt Maria and the next with Aunt Susan. When the rest of my brothers and sisters came to school, my brother Abe and I stayed permanently with Aunt Susan. Aunt Maria chose to board my sisters. I guess that wild boys, as we were, along with our cousin Jake, were a handful.

Abe, my cousin, and I found windows handy for exits when we wanted to do something when we were supposed to be in bed. We also did our share of playing hooky from school. Then too, there was the herdsman's boat and net when we wanted some fun on the water.

The boat, which was usually thrown over a bush to dry, had a hole in the fore-part. A cow had stepped in it and had gone right through. The herdsman used the boat to cross the Samara and Kilshane rivers to swim the herd to pasture. To

14

use the boat we had to sit in the rear, which raised the bow out of the water. Sometimes, in our eagerness to pull the net in when we were fishing, we would crawl too far forward and swamp the boat. Then we would have to undress and dry our clothes so that Aunt Susan wouldn't know what we had been doing. I think she knew anyway, but being good-hearted, she would not scold us. Uncle Jacob would just look at us and grin. We had many good times.

After finishing grade school, we were sent to Chortitza for high school. One year I stayed with my stepmother's sister, Helen Kroeger. The next year, my brother Abe, three other students and I boarded with another widow, also named Kroeger but not related.

In high school we continued to study two languages; besides Russian we could choose between English, French and German. I continued with German but Abe chose French. I have often been grateful for my decision as I have had many opportunities to use German. Abe, not being able to mix with French people, was not able to retain his knowledge. Language is easily forgotten when it is not used.

My family moved several times during our school years. My dad sold his mill in Spaskoya and went northeast about 250 miles to the State of Voronezh. Then they moved to the village of Ostrogozhsk, where Dad started another flour mill and added an oil mill. (Here oil was pressed out of sunflower seeds.) He sold this business to his brother-in-law, George Rempel. Then he went south to Rossosh, where he again built a flour and oil mill. He retained this, and moved to Millerovo.

In Millerovo, there were four flour mills which ground flour for government use only. Dad built a flour and oil mill which ground flour for private persons. He had the only sunflower oil pressing mill there.

I was about to begin my senior year in high school when the family moved to Millerovo. I spent two summers in Millerovo working in a farm machinery factory. During the second summer there was an epidemic of cholera; often people dropped dead on the street. Their faces turned dark immediately.

While this epidemic was raging, I was working in the factory as timekeeper. One day the bookkeeper, whose desk was opposite mine, went out for dinner. He seemed cheerful as he left, but he walked only about a block and fell over dead from cholera.

The same fall there was an epidemic of black pox. This took the lives of my half brothers Nikolai I and Cornelius I, and left my brother Pete and my half brother George with pock marks.

Chapter IV

THE REVOLUTION

I had gone back to Chortitza in 1917 to begin college when the revolution began. A student of three months, I went home to Millerovo for Christmas vacation. Although the revolution was still young, I hardly made it home by train.

Many political parties were already fighting, and while the railroads within political territories were running, sections near territory boundaries had been blown up or had been in some way sabotaged. Chortitza was in Ekaterinoslav territory, and Millerovo was in Don Cossack territory. Having to cross over these boundaries, I had had a difficult time getting home. I should have stayed in Chortitza because being home brought more difficulties for me than transportation had.

When I arrived home I found my family sick with influenza. My dad had been sick for a week by the time I arrived.

The flu epidemic raged all over Russia. One Dutch settlement group, which was called Moloch, consisted of several villages grouped together. In some of these villages, about eighty-five per cent of the population died of the epidemic and the remaining people were too ill to bury their dead. Some people, who came from Chortitza and other villages to help, contracted the illness and died there too. It was so serious that the people were near panic. There were not enough doctors in Russia and people had to try to help themselves.

In the Revolution, the fighting between the Cossacks and the Communists was already very heavy. The Communists were pressing hard to invade the Don Cossack territory and

17

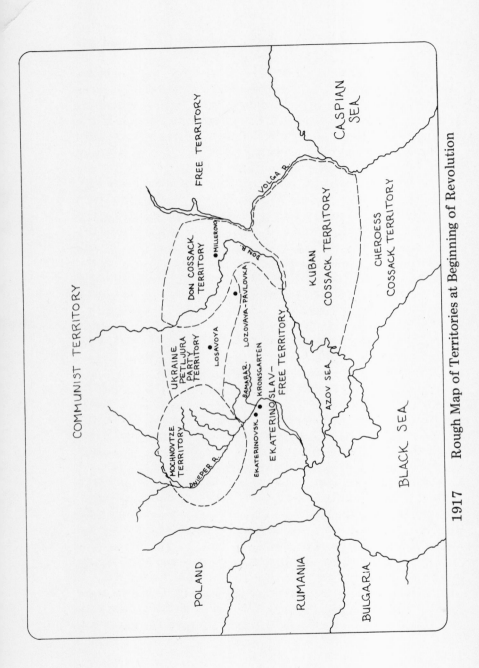

1917   Rough Map of Territories at Beginning of Revolution

the Cossacks needed men from wherever they could get them.

I will pause momentarily here to describe the Cossacks. Americans seem to think that all Russian men are Cossacks who specialize in a difficult dance done from a crouching position. This is not correct. Some clarification may help the person who is not familiar with Russian geography or history to better understand this element of the populace with whom I was fighting during the Revolution.

The Don Cossacks are a clan of Russians who, years ago, were fugitives from Tzarist Russia. They settled in the basin along the River Don. At that time, this clan was fighting the tzar's forces to the north and the Tartars and Turks to the south. The Turks or Tartars would make raids on Cossack villages and take the Cossack women as captives. Then the Cossacks would retaliate with raids on their villages and capture their women. This is how the Cossack blood was intermixed with different nationalities.

The Don Cossacks did not feel related to the Russians or any other nation. They formed a kind of nation of their own within the nation.

When a young Cossack boy became eighteen years of age, he had to report to the induction center of his clan. Here he was trained to ride and fight on horseback. The Cossacks trained the finest horseback riders in the world. When the young Cossack had completed his training, he was sent home on leave for thirty days. After that he was a full-fledged Cossack assigned to the barracks and training all the while.

The Cossack women, with the help of their small children and old men, did practically all the work on their farms. Their families were often smaller than the Russian peasant families because the Cossack men were often away from home fighting for years at a time.

After a while, the Cossack territory was annexed to Russia proper. The tzars then used the fierce Cossack regiments as shock troops. If there was any uprising the Cossacks were sent to squelch it, and squelch it they did. Often, by the time the Cossacks left, the village had been burned and every person and living thing in it killed.* The spoils of any village dealt with belonged to the Cossacks. It was their pay.

The Cossacks have their place in history. It was their forces which harassed Napoleon's army to its death. In World War II, they kept Hitler's armies from advancing to the Russian capital. This, remember, they did on horseback against modern tanks. And even more recently, Premier Khrushchev used the Kalmyk and Kirghiz (slit-eyed people) regiments with units of Cossacks to squelch the Hungarian revolt of the 1950s.

There are three different clans of Cossacks. The Don Cossacks wear a blue uniform with a two-inch red stripe down the side of their trousers. They have red shoulder bars and wear a medium-high sheepskin cap trimmed in gold, with a red top and tassel. They wear a dagger, sword and gun at their sides. They have a special saddle of their own and have their own breed of dark bay horses.

The second clan is the Kuban Cossacks. Their territory extends from the Don Cossack territory south to the Caucasian mountains. These Cossacks are very fierce fighters also. They differ in their dress since their uniform is black. They wear a sort of smock and a tall sheepskin hat. Bullet holders are sewn across their chests. They use a different kind of sword from that used by the Dons; it is shorter, curved, and very flexible and when used, it hisses as it goes through the air.

The Kuban Cossacks also have a distinctive saddle. The seat is very soft and pillow-like. When mounted, the horseman is wedged in and stands in the stirrups all the time. This

* While writing this narrative, in 1964, John took a walk to the downtown business district of our small California community. He went into the five and ten cent store where he met an elderly couple whom he recognized as Russian from their accents. He told me that they had exchanged stories and laughed and talked to him until he related he had been in the Cossack Army. He said that the couple completely froze on him at that point. "This," he said, "shows you how much the Russian people fear the Cossacks." It seems surprising that these people, so far away from Russia, would still respond with fear when learning that they had come in contact with a former Cossack, especially at his age.

Don Cossack

Kuban Cossack

Chercess Cossack

saddle is almost impossible to fall out of. It has two cinches and both a breast and tail harness. Their horses are the reason for this; they are lower in the rear than most horses, almost giraffe-like. Regardless of appearance, these are very hardy horses. They are usually mouse-gray in color.

The third clan is the Chercess Cossacks. Their territory runs south from the Kuban Cossack territory and embraces the Caucasian Mountains. These people are mountaineers; they are tall and fierce. Their uniform is a light-colored smock which extends down to the knees. They, also, wear a high, charcoal-gray sheepskin cap and have bullet holders sewn across the chest of their smocks. They carry a sword, dagger and revolver.

Children of the Chercess clan begin their training at a very early age. A boy at five years of age is taught to use a *kinjal* (dagger). From then on he is taught to ride; particularly he is taught what they call *jigitanka* which is riding on the side, in the front, or under the belly of the horse, "make the scissors" (hold on with the legs), and at the same time shoot or chop with the sword.

The tzars could never conquer these horsemen and lost division after division trying. These Cossacks also used the technique of luring their enemies into valleys and then practically burying them alive by starting an avalanche of rocks tumbling down on them from the top of the mountain.

Because of their urgent need for men for the Revolution, Cossack blood or not, the Cossacks were drafting men who lived in their territory into their forces. I received a draft notice telling me to go to Kamenskoe (Dneprodzerzhinsk) for induction. Kamenskoe is halfway between Millerovo and Rostov on the River Don and was the induction center of the Don Cossack territory.

If I had been in Chortitza, I would have been in free territory and not available for this draft. However, I was in Millerovo and could not return to Chortitza because of the train situation. I had to report. My dad was still delirious from his illness when I left home. I was not to see him again until we met years later in Canada.

I took the train to Kamenskoe. At the induction center

24

there, I claimed my rights as a Mennonite to be a conscientious objector. I was laughed at, and informed that such rights were over when the Revolution started. Since I was living in Cossack territory, I was, at that moment, a Cossack and would have to be trained as a Cossack.

There was no time to give extensive training so I received a short, but concentrated, course in becoming a horseman. I had to learn to ride as only a Cossack could ride—as if horse and rider were one.

There was another Mennonite boy named Frank Frantz inducted with me. He came from Kamenskoe where his father was also a miller. We were the only two Mennonites inducted at that particular time, but we were later joined by others.

I fought with the Cossacks against the Communists for about three months. While fighting on the border of Don Cossack territory, we captured some young Cossacks who had deserted the Cossacks and joined the Communist party. Desertion into any other army is, in the Cossack mind, treason—punishable by death. We were told not to kill these young men. They were sent along the fighting lines until their parents were found.

Because the territory was being heavily besieged by the Communists and the Cossacks needed fighting men desperately, the Cossack women had come out to help fight in the lines with their men. The freedom of their territory meant a great deal to them.

When one or both of the prisoner's parents were found in the lines, the father would rise with the mother beside him and say, "We gave you life and we take it." Then the son, kneeling down, was beheaded; usually with one stroke of the sword. The mother would stand there silently crying and crossing herself, being an Orthodox Catholic. I witnessed this about five times. It made me sick. I could not eat for days afterward.

I decided to leave the territory and go south. I left the Cossack Army one night when we were fighting close to Lugansk (Vorochlovgrad) which was close to the Ukrainian border. Snow and rain were falling intermittently. I traveled by foot along the railroad. I would go home to Millerovo and get some clothes; then I must take a train to go to Kronsgarten. When I arrived at home my stepmother was in the yard. I spoke to her for a few minutes but did not tell her my plans. If I did not tell anyone what I was doing, no one could tell on me.

Our Millerovo home was comprised of one big house with a duplex house adjacent. One-half of the duplex was for the head miller's family and the other half, closest to the big house, was for the boys of the family. I got my clothes and left for the railroad station.

At the railroad station I was told to pay the conductor when I got off; nobody knew how far the train would get. I was going to Aunt Susan's in Kronsgarten, which usually would be an overnight trip. After three days, I had only traveled as far as Lozavaya.* At Lozavaya the Ukraina Petljura Party, which held this territory, arrested me.

I was taken to an ordinary house, which was serving as a jail, and placed in a room about twelve feet by twelve feet. There were nearly fifty other prisoners in it. The room was without furniture and was unbelievably filthy. Since no toilet facilities were provided, the corners were used, but in the crowding, the filth was trampled all over the floor.

Men were called out of this room by name and questioned. New prisoners were often brought in. Some were called out and never returned; others returned from questioning miserably beaten. I remember one man who returned with one of his eyeballs hanging out of his head. Tension was great among the prisoners. We all wondered who would be called next. Each hoped it would not be he.

When it was my turn, I was questioned at length. I suppose I was suspected of spying. I was questioned for three days. During my beatings, the bridge of my nose was broken when I was hit in the face with the butt of a rifle. I was already endowed with a generous nose. With the bridge broken I was left with a beak-like appendage.

Beaten, half-starved, and in my underwear, I was taken out

*We believe this is Lozavaya-Povlovka. S. M. D.

with about fifteen other prisoners. It was winter and the snow was crusted. The soldiers were dressed heavily in sheepskin coats and heavy boots. We were marched to a big ditch about twenty feet long and eight feet deep. I saw some bodies lying there in grotesque forms. I also saw one man lying in a corner, half covered with snow, moving and moaning. We were lined up at the edge of the ditch so that when we were shot we would fall into the ditch.

It was cloudy; now the moon was shining—now it was not. When the cloud passed, the moon was very clear and the air very still and cold.

By this time I cared little about what happened to me. The soldiers shot a volley, but after the rifles cracked I found myself still standing and not hurt. I started running, barefooted in the crusted snow, with the soldiers shouting in pursuit. They shot again, but were poor shots and missed me again. The moon went under the clouds which made visibility difficult for them. They were also encumbered by their heavy clothing while I could move quickly, being so scantily dressed.

I had run for about half a mile, when I heard someone coming behind me. I tried to run faster, but my lungs were afire from the cold air. When I could not go any farther, I threw myself on a snowdrift and waited for the shot. Then I looked behind me and saw that another half-naked man had followed me. He too had escaped the bullets. He said, "Come on," and pulled me up by my arms. He saved my life by insisting that I continue, for if I had stopped there, I would have frozen to death.

His name was Andrays. He was an older man than I. Andrays told me that he had been going south, too, when he was caught. (If he told me what he was doing in the north, I have forgotten.) It was now, NOW that counted. The past was not important. He was single too. There is little else that I can tell you about Andrays except that he was a Lutheran German.

The Mennonites referred to the Lutheran Germans as the Prussians. There were quite a few Prussian villages in the Ukraine and in the southeastern part of the country as far as the Volga River. You could always tell when you were in a Lutheran village since their homes were mostly made of adobe and almost all of them were painted blue. They, like us, were farmers.

Andrays and I started walking toward the next village. To our left, on the horizon, we saw telephone poles. Telephone poles generally follow the road. Being fugitives, we dared not be seen on the road, but we could follow in the direction of the poles. As we approached the village we saw lights. Outside the village was a lone house. After much deliberation, we gathered our courage and approached it.

A little old peasant woman came to the door. She nearly slammed the door on us when she saw us, but Andrays did not let her. We explained to her that we meant her no harm, but that we were very cold. She could plainly see that we were in trouble. We begged her for some bread and clothes. She produced some pants, coats and boots which she said belonged to her husband who had died only a short time before. They were, by far, too big for us, but they were warm and certainly better than we had. She told us that soldiers were in the village, so we decided to keep moving; it was then about one o'clock in the morning.

As we moved out of the village, we heard the soldiers shouting and moving our way. We were sure that the officials had telephoned ahead of us from Lozavaya. There was a straw stack nearby, and we ran toward it. The peasant farmer had left some loose straw lying around the stack when he had plucked the straw for evening stable bedding. We lay down and covered ourselves with it. I could hear the soldiers coming near and tried to lie perfectly still. I was cold and scared. I could hear my heart beating and shaking the straw which scared me all the more.

The soldiers stood there near the stack listening. Before us stretched the steppes. (Sound carries very far across the flat prairie-like country through the cold thin air.) The soldiers had a dog with them; he came up to us, and sniffed at us, but made no noise. The soldiers were watching him. The dog walked up to where I was lying, lifted his hind leg and wet on me. Being so sparsely covered with the straw, I got it right in my face. Then I heard one soldier say something about being cold, and then something about going back to play poker. Soon they left.

After awhile, we got up and started walking again in a generally southern direction. We really did not know where we were, but we knew we had to put distance between ourselves and the soldiers. We traveled from then on mostly at night, stealing food and better-fitting clothes and boots when we had a chance.

In some of the clothes which we stole, there were some rationing cards for food and clothes. Having no money, we could not buy anything; but the blue seals on these cards were to be of use to us later on in our escape. I do not know why we did not throw them away, but it was lucky for us that we didn't.

Andrays and I walked and ran about 350 miles in thirteen days and nights. Running helped keep us warm so we ran a lot. It seems to me now that we ran most of the way. When we reached the Samara River, we could find no way to cross except by one bridge. The Petljurovtze forces held the bridge and it was guarded.

We traveled both up and down river trying to find a boat to steal but could find none. If we approached the bridge and the two sentries determined that we were not authorized, we would be shot.

We decided to watch the bridge for a day to familiarize ourselves with the routine. Then cold and hungry, we decided to risk trying to cross the bridge. The river was too big to swim, especially in such cold weather.

We approached the sentry and showed him our stolen ration cards. This sentry called the other sentry to come and look at our papers. They both examined the cards. One said to the other in a half-tone, "Look, it has the blue seal. It must be official." I was never so glad to meet two men who could not read. We were permitted to cross.

We dared not hurry or in any way look suspicious, else we might have been shot in the back. As soon as we thought we were out of sight, we ran toward the river bottom and into the safety of the woods.

The next day was warmer and it started to thaw. We kept plodding along until we came to a territory where we did not have to be so careful. We were about fifty miles from Kronsgarten. Here three rivers come together; the small river, the Kilshane, runs into the Samara, which in turn empties into the Dnieper. This was the territory I had played in as a child. I had fished in all three rivers and played in the woods when my cousins and I had played hooky from school. Now I was really anxious to complete my journey.

Andrays and I parted at the village of Josephstal. I never saw him again. I have forgotten where he was going, but I faintly recollect that he said it was only halfway for him.

Alone now, I continued until I came to the little river Kilshane. By then the thaw had swollen the river. I went to the place where we used to ford the river, but it was too deep. I had to swim it. The water was unbelievably cold. I hurried up the hill and traveled the mile beyond to the woods where Aunt Susan Rempel lived. I was home at last.

When I got to the house, it was getting dark. No one was home so I climbed in the window. When I had roomed here during my school years, we had often sneaked in and out. It was a handy entrance now. I was dead tired, so I climbed into the familiar bed.

About one o'clock in the morning my cousin Jake woke me quietly. He told me that the Communists, who held this territory, had plundered the village the day before and that five people had been killed. That was the reason everybody was in hiding.

I stayed then with Aunt Susan and Uncle Jacob for about six months. Whenever a raiding party of Communists came, they would ask who I was. My aunt and uncle would inform them that I was a hired man.

Before I had returned, the farmers had been hiding their thirty-five horses in the woods. They continued to do this while I was there, taking turns tending them. The raiders usually came to villages and confiscated the best horses either to ride or to pull their ammunition wagons. Our villagers wanted to save their best young stock which they did for a

30

year. They were finally lost, however.

Usually during these raids the family would be lined up in the house against the wall. Then the hired girl and I would be called into the house and the soldiers would start abusing and making fun of the family. For example, they would shoot into the wall near someone's head, and then say, "See how this bloodsucker kulak cringes when shot at," or some similar statement which made sport of the defenseless people. To save my own skin, I had to pretend that I was enjoying it. The hired man, the lower class, was supposed to enjoy seeing his superiors mistreated.

Near the end of my six-month stay in Kronsgarten, a Communist raiding party came through and gathered all the men into one house. My cousin, young Jake Rempel, was among these. I was in the woods at the time tending the horses with fifteen other men. A special collection had been taken at the church for the maintenance of the cemetery. A raiding party had come through earlier in the week and had taken this money.

That day the raiding party demanded the collection from the minister, Uncle Jacob, who was the only minister in the small church. He told them that it had already been taken, but they would not believe him. They made him leave with two soldiers to go to his home. As he knelt in the front room of his home, having opened the safe, he was shot through the forehead. The bullet passed through his head, hit the top of the safe, ricocheted off the wall and embedded itself in the sofa.

The soldiers dragged his body out into the front yard and forbade anyone to bury him. There he lay for three days. He was beginning to decompose, so when I returned, my cousin Jake and I stole out in the night and buried him.*

We learned that Makhno's bandits had gone on one raid in

* We note a slight disagreement. Mr. Rempel's daughter states that her father was buried by the men of the village after funeral services on December 11, 1918. S. M. D.

the village of No. 4 Dubovka in the settlement of Yasikovo,† where they rounded up all the men, twelve years old and over, and placed them in a cellar. Then they hand grenaded the building and cellar until all inside were killed. The women and children were then taken away. No one knew what had become of them. The village itself was burned to the ground. Only the chimneys of some of the houses remained as accusing fingers pointing to heaven. This was done because the villagers had organized to defend themselves against such raids.

Later, when the Communists came to Kronsgarten and gathered the village elders in one house, we feared that they were getting ready to kill them. About fifteen of the village boys gathered outside the house and started shooting to get their attention. When the six Communists came out of the house to see what was happening, we shot them. Coming from the lighted rooms they acted as if they could not see very well in the outside darkness. Then we loaded their corpses into a wagon and took them to where the Samara River joined the Dnieper, and floated their bodies.

The Communists came to the village days later looking for their comrades. They started asking questions. They were suspicious because they returned every day, looking all over, asking questions and beating people.

It began to get pretty hot for the fifteen of us, so we took to the woods and became fugitives. We stayed in the woods for about three and a half months.

The woods were a little more than half a mile over the hill from Kronsgarten. They extended on both sides of the Samara River for a width of about six miles, and upstream for about a hundred miles. I went only as far as thirty-five miles during these days of hiding. The trees were dense and offered an excellent hiding place for our group.

There were twenty-five or thirty ancient, hollow willow trees in the woods near Kronsgarten which we knew about

† Yasikovo (sometimes spelled Jasikovo) is the Russian name for a Dutch settlement which consisted of five villages: No. 1 Nikolaipol, No. 2 Varvarovka, No. 3 Dolinovka, No. 4 Dubovka, and No. 5 Morosovo.

from playing there as children. These offered us individual hiding places. I claimed the tree closest to Kronsgarten on the same side of the river. Some of the boys hid in trees on the other side of the river, and some, a little to the north. I made narrow slits in my tree from which I could see in all directions. Sometimes the Communists rode very close by looking for us, and we were afraid. Once a platoon was sent to look for us.

One of our boys was caught, hung by the feet, and a fire built under him so that he was burned alive. We missed him and went looking for him; several days later we found him. When we were sure it was safe we sneaked up and cut him down. His hands were burned off close to the elbows and his head was burned beyond recognition. His clothes had burned the rest of his body very badly. We could hardly touch him as the flesh would come off of his bones. Thus we learned what our fate could be if any of the rest of us were caught.

One day I was hungry and came out of the woods. As I came sneaking around Aunt Susan's barn, I saw a Communist raiding party there looting. They had Aunt Susan out in the yard. I leaned my rifle against the back corner of the barn before I showed myself. The soldiers asked Aunt Susan who I was and she said I was the hired man and that I had been out chopping wood. I calmly walked to the horse barn and out the back door. I grabbed my rifle and peppered them. They ran away leaving all that they had looted.

Now the heat was really on. A Communist unit was sent out of Ekaterinoslav* to search for us in the woods. We had to hide very carefully so that we would not be caught. They combed the woods twice looking for us, but none of our boys were caught.

I decided then to join the Republican army and fight the Communists. A unit of the Republican army was at Novomoskovsk at that time. I said goodbye to Aunt Susan and the family. Everyone was crying when I left, which made it harder for me to leave.

* This city is found on early maps as Yekaterinoslav. On later maps it is shown as Ekaterinoslav but is currently shown as Dnepropetrovsk.

I could have saved myself the trip because the next day the unit came right back through Kronsgarten. I found Henry Penner in my group and also other Mennonite boys whom I knew. Penner and I were together through all our fighting days and even came to the United States together some time later.

After fighting with the Republican army for a while, our unit got mixed up with my original Cossack regiment. The Cossacks demanded me back and I was transferred. Henry Penner and some of the other boys from our village were also transferred, although they had not been with the Cossacks before. I met Frank Frantz again, and we fought together for a time.

One day we were being badly shelled as we were flanking the tanks. A shell came my way which killed my horse and sent us plummeting down together. I was not seriously injured, but blood came out of my eyes, nose and ears and I was left dazed. Frantz saw me go down and later told my parents that I was dead; he had seen me die. My parents held funeral services for me then for the first time.

The Anarchist army, under the leadership of Makhno, was caught in a squeeze between three armies. To get out of this squeeze, Makhno decided to join our army. We were the only unit going north toward the Dnieper River where they wanted to go.

The Anarchists had no religion. Anarchist means anti-Christ.* These soldiers lived for wine and women, and they killed and plundered for fun. They killed people by the hundreds. These Anarchists did so much killing that the people of the whole Ukraine feared them. (This was not a group anyone would be proud to have traveled with.)

After the Anarchist army joined our army, our commanding officers thought that there should be more order in their ranks. They appointed some commissioned men and some noncommissioned men to lead them. I happened to be chosen a sergeant. This was a tough assignment as these

* Anarch (Greek *anarchos*, without a leader; *an*, without; *archon*, leader), taken by Mr. Dyck to mean, without divine leadership.

troops did not know any discipline.

We were getting close to the Dnieper River where the Anarchist army wanted to go. One evening I was told to put out some sentries from my unit. When I read the names of three Anarchists, one tried to draw his gun on me. I had developed what others considered a peculiar method of gun handling. When drawing my pistol or aiming my rifle, I position my middle finger in the trigger and lay my index finger along the barrel. The reasoning behind this is that a person points his index finger very accurately while swinging around to point at the target. I do not suggest that others try this, however, as it is also an excellent way to shoot yourself in the leg while learning. I was faster than my Anarchist adversary and shot him through the shoulder. The rest of my squad stood and looked at me for a few moments and then slowly dispersed.

The next morning when I got up, I had no soldiers. I went to headquarters to report losing my troops and found another sergeant there beaten and bloody. While I was there, others arrived in similar condition. We were a pitiful group— four sergeants, one lieutenant, and one captain and no troops. All had deserted us during the night. We were all glad that they had not killed us as they left. Since they had left me unharmed, I assumed that my display of sharpshooting had convinced them that it might not be safe to try to sneak up on me. After that, we were all transferred to a division under General Markov. I remained with this division until the end of the Revolution.

Killing and war are not the natural way of life. There are times, even in war and revolution, when warriors abandon their roles as soldiers and just become young men again. This happened to me at least once, and I do not know whether to credit the incident to quick thinking or to just plain luck. I was on patrol at night. Suddenly, on the top of a hill I found myself rifle-to-rifle with a soldier of the Red army. It happened so suddenly that neither of us were prepared for the encounter. There was a moment of silence with my heart jumping. I must have grinned and said something foolish, because my adversary relaxed his grip on his rifle. I said something like, "Let's don't shoot each other. Let's sit down and have a smoke together like friends." And that is what we did. We sat and smoked and talked. After a time we shook hands and departing in peace, returned to our own respective sides of a revolution which neither of us had asked to be a part of. The only advantage to fighting a war against your countrymen is that when a meeting like this happens, at least you can understand the language of the other and get away with it.

I *was* wounded; but I didn't even know it. It was winter and I had ridden at night to the home of a friend. Sometime during my visit someone noticed blood on my leg. I rolled up my pants and found a bullet hole clean through the lower part of the calf of my leg. Apparently a stray bullet had hit me or a sniper had shot at me, and in the extreme cold, I hadn't felt it. There was no harm done, but it left a small scar to show my grandchildren to prove to them that I had been in a war.

I was called the Russian equivalent of "Quarter" by my fighting comrades. I acquired this nickname because of a splotch of dark hair, the size of a quarter, which stood out against my light-colored hair. I see this mark of distinction today, passed on to one grandson. He carries only a dime's worth of my quarter, however.

In the second year of the Revolution after I had left Kronsgarten and returned to the Republican (White) army, the Communists arrested my dad and the other four mill owners in Millerovo. These five men were put aboard a train in a boxcar. There they were beaten and probably presumed dead. Unconscious, they were kicked out of the moving train. Three were killed. Only my dad and Mr. Shroeder survived.

They were discovered about fifteen miles from Millerovo. It was winter and when word came that Dad had been found, my brothers, Abe, then about eighteen years old, and Pete, about thirteen, went after him with a child's hand-sled and brought him home.

Dad had been so badly beaten that the skin on his back was left extremely thin and scarred as if burned. Even thirty-five years later when he visited me in Ohio, a fold in a sheet would make his back bleed. It took him three or four months to recover enough to pursue his business.

The reader may wonder what provoked such treatment. These five millers were of the middle class. People of the middle class were called "kulaks" meaning "the fist." "The fist" refers to the practice of hitting with the fist any underling, such as a hired man, who didn't obey. The fist was the punishment and both the rich and the kulaks dealt it out. The Dutch did not use this kind of treatment too often, but it was common practice for the Russian rich or middle class.

When the Communists took over, they tried to turn the class system completely upside down, with the poor on top and the rich and middle class at the bottom. All those of respect were shamed and scorned. To the Communists the kulaks were considered unfit to live. Children of the kulaks and the rich often were not permitted to attend school. Children permitted to attend school were encouraged to be disrespectful and taunt their teachers. This resulted in the loss of many of Russia's fine teachers.

The Communists confiscated all Dad had, his mills and his home. Dad fled with his family back to Kronsgarten and stayed with Aunt Susan in the summer of 1919.

As the revolution continued, the people could not plow or plant crops. There was a constant change of armies in and out of the villages. The food-procuring officers confiscated practically all produce; horses and cows were taken. The farmers were left without even seed to plant. There was no importing or exporting since the borders were sealed off. The armies had to feed their troops, so the citizens went hungry.

Famine developed all over Russia, but things were especially bad in Communist-occupied territory. The Communists did not seem to understand that they were cutting off their own supplies.

The winters were very severe and almost no one had enough clothing to keep warm. Epidemics of cholera and typhus started and hundreds of people died. The ground was frozen deep, so corpses were put in sheds awaiting spring burial.

The people were hungry and when the hunger had continued for months and months, they became desperate. They started to break into the dead-body sheds and take arms or legs of corpses to cook for their families. Sentries were placed by these sheds, but still people would dig in from behind the shed to get at the dead. For a time I stood four-hour-daily sentry duty at one of these sheds, and witnessed this happening.

Throughout the revolution, the people of Russia, including my family, endured many terrible hardships and atrocities. This narrative does not intend to indicate that atrocities and hardships were peculiar to those living in territories held by any political army in particular. Crimes of inhumanity were committed against peoples in all territories by soldiers of all the armies. Those mentioned here are only ones which I witnessed or which I learned about from my family and friends.

Being in Communist territory, my particular family suffered mostly at the hands of Communists. Forces from both sides passed through villages, as battles were won and lost daily, and villages and territories changed hands with the battles. Always there was the search for food and clothing. Women were often molested since sadistic men are in any army; their politics or uniforms make no difference.

In one instance, one raiding party came into the village of Prijut (Yakovlevka). They demanded money, clothes and any valuable items. There had been so many raids before that there was nothing to give, but the raiders continued to insist.

In one home they raped the women while the rest of the family was lined up against the wall and forced to watch. Then one soldier stuck his sword through the stomach of the baby in the cradle. He held it up on his sword. The baby could not cry, but only gasped for breath. As he held it in the air, another soldier proceeded to chop off its feet and hands.

The father and mother then forgot their fear and threw themselves at their assailants. Each was struck in the head with the butt of a rifle and knocked unconscious. Then the soldier calmly dropped the dead baby off of his sword and onto the floor.

Incidents like this happened all over the Ukraine. It is easy enough to understand why some of the Mennonites, who are a non-resisting people, lost faith in their church doctrines or at least questioned their religion.

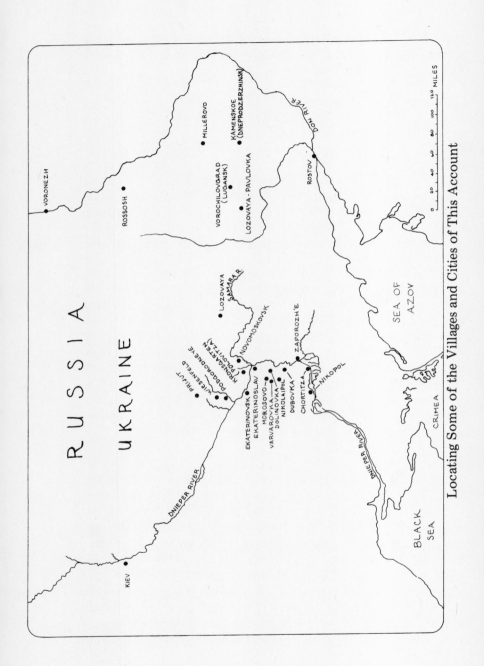

Locating Some of the Villages and Cities of This Account

40

Chapter V

THE FAMILY IN THE REVOLUTION

I am not going to elaborate on where I was or what I was doing during these years. We were constantly on the move, fighting all day and traveling all night to the next battle. Often the kitchens supplying our food did not catch up with us for days. The soldiers from all armies had to go into the countryside and raid the citizens for supplies. We took what we needed; we had to if we were to continue fighting.

When I left home we all still lived in the town of Millerovo located in the Don Cossack territory. The Communists had confiscated everything Father owned—even clothes. There was no logic to anything being done in those days. The local Communists did not understand what Communism was or anything else. All they knew was that they could rob, kill, and plunder anybody and anything legally. The whole country was a mess in every respect.

I asked my sister Agatha to write an account of our family during my absence. My sister's writing begins in Millerovo where my family shared the fate of many others.

"From Millerovo, in the fall of 1919, Father fled with his family, trying to get south to the Mennonite settlements. Here it may be proper to explain the rush to leave Millerovo.

"Dad had a German-made, 350 horsepower coal-and-gas-run engine to run the flour mill. It was a complicated thing which consisted of a sealed furnace which burned hard coal. The hard coal smoldered in this furnace which was about eighteen feet high and about eighteen feet in diameter. Gas was piped through four-foot pipes to a filter cooler twenty feet around and twenty feet high. The gas had to go through a compartment of water, then through a compartment of wood shavings, and finally through a layer of charcoal. From here it went to the engine. To start this monstrosity, Dad had a small engine run by kerosene. This was used to start the big engine for the air compressor. The kerosene engine provided the power for all the lights in the flour and sunflower oil mills and was the power for the lights in the houses and yards. There was no city lighting system.

"Because of his experience with these engines, Dad was a specialist. The Communist government ordered him to supervise all the engines of that kind from Millerovo down to the Caucasian Mountains. Dad had an engineer to run his engines. He sent him to supervise the repairs but the engineer could not get all of the engines to work. Some of the engines were worn out and it was impossible to get parts. The Communists said that he was sabotaging them and the engineer was shot.

"The supervisor, under the Communists, was held responsible for any breakdown and made to pay for it with his life, even if he were miles away when the breakdown occurred. The cream of Russia's mechanics, engineers, doctors, and farmers were wiped out in this manner. In a collective farm, if the crop failed because of weather or anything else, the supervisor lost his life. Knowing this, Dad feared a similar fate. This prompted him to flee.

"It happened that a Baptist minister and his family were hiding in a boxcar which was pulled over on a railroad siding waiting for a south-bound train. This man was a friend of Dad's and he implored Dad to go along while there was a chance. Dad finally agreed.

"We left our home in secret and sneaked into that freight car at night. We couldn't take much with us, but we did not have much to take anyway. We managed to leave with some cooking utensils, some bedding, and a few books and pictures. It was in this manner that we left Millerovo and returned to Ekaterinoslav, the territory where we originated.

"Our cousin, Dietrich Rempel, came for us and took us to Kronsgarten to our Aunt Susan's home. It was about an eighteen-mile trip. We stayed there from the fall of 1919 to the spring of 1920. Then we moved to No. 1 Nikolaipol. I have to explain that these settlements were mentioned by numbers, "1," "2," "3," and "4," by the Dutch. They had

42

official Russian names however.

"In the spring of 1920, my family rented a small farm known as the old Cornelius Friesen homestead which was adjacent to the schoolhouse. Cornelius Friesen was dead, but his son had lived on the property for a while. He, too, had had to go into hiding which is why it was available for us. Cornelius II's sons lived on the next property.

"I should make it clear that the people in the village knew that Dad was in hiding. The Communists could tell that the Friesen place was occupied, but as long as it was not the missing Cornelius Friesen family living there and the Communists did not know that Dad was being sought in another location, all was well.

"On this farm there were about ten acres of seeded rye. The year before no one had bothered to cut it so it had seeded itself. We cut the grain with Mr. Friesen's harvester. It was an old machine. One person had to drive the horses in front, and the other person had to rake and cut the rye off the platform with a fork. We shocked it and left it to age.

"We could not get a wagon right away to bring in our harvest. A few days later we drove up to get it and discovered with horror that someone had beaten the grain out and stolen it. Only the straw was left. This was a serious loss for us since we had counted on it for our winter bread.

"In addition to this, the Communists made frequent raids on the villages under the pretext of looking for guns. During their searches they took whatever food they found. Dad had hidden a half-bushel of barley in the attic, which we would have used both for bread and seed. This was found and taken, leaving us nothing for winter and no seed for the spring.

"We had secured a cow, but it was necessary to keep her in the cellar. We could not keep her in the barn since someone would certainly have stolen her. Without other food to sustain us, we were forced to butcher her during the winter of 1920. This meat did not last very long. Under government instructions, whenever Red soldiers came to the village, the citizens had to give them room and board. With these extras to feed, our meat was gone before our need for winter food was over.

"We started to prepare the lower fields for planting the

43

next year, having bought a little seed. We had completed the firing of the weeds when the Communists measured the land and divided it among the Russian peasants. That year we had only a small garden to work.

"One day Susan and I heard what sounded like sticks beating on a wash tub. We climbed to the top of the mill to see what was happening. We could see the Bolsheviks and the Cossacks fighting. The field was full of bodies and blood. We descended very quietly since we did not wish to be discovered and shot as spies.

"Dad and Abe worked as cabinet makers through those winters. They sold their work for food. They earned barely enough food to keep us alive.

"All kindness was not dead, however. A widow neighbor, at great risk, was still hiding her cow in her cellar. She provided cottage cheese and whey for our family which helped to sustain us. After a while, however, the cow went dry. There was no way to breed her since all other cattle in the area had been taken away, so the cow had to be butchered in the cellar and eaten secretly.

"By the end of 1920, we were already greatly weakened by the confiscation of our goods, food, clothing, and livestock, and further reduced by an epidemic of typhus. The year 1921 brought the final blow—drought. The drought robbed us of all means of survival. There was little to harvest. Thus the famine with all its awesome consequences started.

"Now the time had come for something drastic to be done. We had no food and no money. Money was useless to everybody except government officials and party members, anyway. In 1921, sister Katherina traveled to Ekaterinovka* to stay with our married sister, Susan, and her husband, Jacob Driediger. Our two older brothers, Abram and Pete, left home, traveling on foot, to go to the village of Prijut where our maternal aunts lived. Aunt Liz was married to Peter

* North and west of the city of Ekaterinoslav, along the Dnieper River, is the smaller city of Ekaterinovka. Current maps show Dneprodzerzhinsk (Kamenskoe).

Neufeld, and Aunt Susan to Jacob Neufeld. They were sisters married to brothers.

"The first day the boys made it to the city of Ekaterinoslav. They went to the home of a Jewish tailor who for years had traveled from village to village and from house to house to tailor suits for the men. All the Mennonite villagers knew him as Tailor Heinrich. This man took our brothers into his house and gave them supper which consisted of one fish (pickled herring), one onion, and a slice of bread. A cup of tea warmed the meal. He let the boys stay overnight and gave them breakfast before allowing them to begin the next lap of their journey. The breakfast was one slice of bread, one onion, and a cup of tea.

"Thus fortified, the boys started to walk the fifteen miles to Kronsgarten. There they stayed with Aunt Susan Rempel overnight. The next day they began the journey to Wiesenfeld which was twenty-five miles further. Here Dad's stepsister's family, the Heinrich Klassens, lived. Fortunately, Dad's stepbrother, Abraham Neufeld, (there are Neufelds on both sides of our parents' families) was visiting the Klassens that day. He lived in Prijut, and gave the boys a ride. These three families of Neufelds were neighbors in a new settlement. Hopefully there would be more food there. The boys stayed with Peter's and Jacob's families from spring, 1921 until early 1922. Our half brother, Nikolai II, was born during the winter of 1921.

"The year 1922 inherited a sad and heavy burden from its predecessor. The famine increased steadily and reached its climax in the months of March and April. In January of 1922, we lost our little stepbrother Cornelius II. Our preacher, Abraham Quiering, from No. 3 Dolinovka, brought each of us a bun (like a zwieback) when he came to visit us. We were all in poor condition from lack of food. Brother Cornelius was four years old. His arms and legs were like broomsticks and his stomach was bloated, indicating the last stages of starvation. He broke his bun in half and put the other half on the shelf saying, 'I'll eat that next day.' 'Next day' never came for him. His intestines could not tolerate the food and the good Lord took him home. He was too far gone from starvation. May God have mercy on those who must die in this way.

"From that time on, Dad and Mother were very somber and withdrawn. They prayed constantly and asked the Lord for help and His promise of eternal life. The fall and winter of 1921 had left their marks on our bodies and hearts.

"One day our parents called us into the living room. Only three of us were at home then; George, then eleven, Nick, about one year old, and I, who was nineteen. When we went into the room, I knew that they were worried. Both were weeping. Father started by saying, 'Let us get on our knees and call on the living God.

> 'May the dear God show Himself as a living God and Father and help us from starvation. But if it is Your will, give us Your grace to shorten our suffering and take us to you. Strengthen our faith, so we won't despair in the love You had for us on the cross.'

"Then Mother prayed her simple supplication. I prayed silently with them. So we left everything in the hands of God. I have never heard our parents as discouraged as they were then.

"In the spring, Abram and Pete came back home to stay. Uncle Peter Neufeld brought them back on a wagon; at least they did not have to walk. The boys were an additional burden for our parents to worry about. They meant two more hungry stomachs which would be empty.

"Father and Abram worked long hours on the joiners' bench trying to earn some wages. They made spinning wheels, repaired wagons and made sandals. The sandals had soles of wood and linen straps. Mother made shoes with leather and linen and gave others instructions. Our parents gave all their strength to our survival; very often they came close to collapse.

"Father made a lathe with manual drive (foot-driven) on which he made many spinning wheels. He adjusted the knife (cutting blade) and Abram provided the power. Abe kept the lathe running all day long with only simple soup to give him strength.

Sandal Making

"One day Abram had to drive to the city of Ekaterinoslav to make a delivery. He was returning home when the horse collapsed. There was nothing he could do but walk the three miles home and report this misfortune to our parents. After a few hours the horse recovered his strength and came home. There was no choice but to slaughter him. We ate all the meat, even the hide. We cut the hide into small pieces, put them in boiling water and then ran them through a grinder. The poor horse was more bone than meat.

"That spring, for two or three weeks we caught gophers for food, but after that there were no more to be caught, and again there was no food to eat.

"One day, Johann Sawatzky, from our village No. 3 Dolinovka, brought us a large loaf of rye bread. With tears in their eyes, our parents accepted the bread. They divided it into little pieces for each of us, and we existed for another week.

"Another time, a Lutheran man came to order some work or repair. He saw our tomcat and made a swap. For our tomcat, we got a goose. We also got some potato peels from Jakob Patkaus. It was a very important day for us.

"We grew silkworms that spring. We fed the worms leaves from the mulberry trees for two months until they made cocoons. To make the silk we collected the cocoons, put them in boiling water (to loosen the threads), and then unwound the cocoons. We wound the thread, catching it on a little broom wisp. Mother spun thread for sewing and knitting. We sold some for a living. She could only get as much flour as our ball of thread was big. That work was nothing to live on.

"The soft heart of my girl friend Maria Klassen (no relation), who lived east of us, warmed toward us and she came to our aid. Her parents had been murdered in No. 4 Dubovka by the Machnovse bands. She lived with her two brothers and one sister. Maria worked in a cheese factory which belonged to the Red Government. The whey which was left over after making the cheese was supposed to be taken to the pig growers. Maria, knowing our plight, brought us one and a half gallons of whey in secret at night twice a week. We divided it into three parts. There was a little for every day. She brought this to us for about three weeks until, all of a sudden, suspicion arose and she had to stop. May our Lord reward her with His blessing for her kindness.

"After the whey we had nothing of sustenance for three weeks. With the pressing need for food, Abram and I went begging in the Russian villages. While begging, Abram received two small pastries made from Russian thistle and mustard seed oil. He gave me one-half of one because I hadn't gotten anything from my day of begging. He ate the other half. He took one pastry home. Our father tried to eat part of it but he could not swallow it; it was too bitter. He put it aside, but hunger forced him back again. He bit into it but again he could not swallow it. He tried again and again.

"Many people died. I saw them myself as they lay dead on the steps when we were begging.

"We had saved cabbage stems in the fall for fuel instead of straw. The cabbage stems gave more heat. We burned this in our oven, and it warmed our kitchen.

"By spring of 1922 we were weak from hunger. I remember one day when Peter and George sat on the oven bench (Note: this probably refers to a massive clay structure where the flue heated the whole installation. Sometimes people slept in a cubicle provided on top) and warmed themselves. I asked them to move closer together; I too wanted to sit on the warm bench but the boys did not move. They had no strength left in them. They could not even close their lips. Their mouths were open. This frightened me and I moved on. There was no crying, no laughing or arguing in the house.

"We were saved in our darkest hour, by our brothers in faith in America. God had answered our prayers. Our family received the first American help in April, 1922. A food box arrived from Melinda Zimmerly of Dalton, Ohio, with whom you were staying. The box contained some sugar, wheatlet, corn meal and cocoa.

"One week later we received another parcel from you, Brother John. The contents of this box were the same as the preceding one except that there was a little more of each item. The parcel was a double blessing for us because through it we

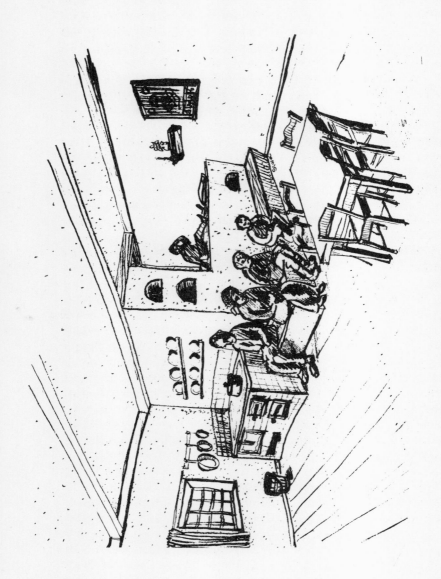

Oven Bench

learned that you were alive and well. Both from reports from others serving with you in the army and from not receiving any word of your whereabouts for several years, we had presumed you were dead and had held several funeral services for you.

"When we received these and other parcels from you and your friends in America, our hearts thanked God and our fellow man for willingness to share with us.

"In April, the American Soup Kitchens, administered by Herbert Hoover, were opened. In the beginning only children were fed, but soon adults received nourishment, also. Although the kitchens could not provide for all the hungry people, large numbers were helped, and steadily the numbers of deaths from starvation declined. In the month of May, we received more American help in the form of food and clothing. There was flour to bake buns (Note: this was probably yeast dough) for the whole village. This was received from the Committee for Baking. Everyone received, as a daily ration, one bun and one cup of cocoa; the next day, one bun and one cup of bean soup; the third day, one bun and one cup of corn meal porridge. This happened in May, June, and to the end of July. Only an eyewitness could have an idea of the joy and gratitude showing on the faces of the suffering, emaciated people.

"During June and July the number of persons receiving meals increased until nearly sixty percent of the population was being helped. All of us saw the immensity of the American aid. Assured by the Bible that God works in mysterious ways to provide for His children, we knew that we had felt the warmth of His hand. May He reward our brothers and sisters in America for their life-saving help, received in our hour of need.

"We were among those receiving relief from the American Mennonite Relief. We received help for a whole year until we could provide for ourselves in June, 1923. The relief kitchens continued in the Ukraine until August 1, 1923. Other help was received in the form of tractors, horses, and clothing. The American Mennonite Church ended all help in the Ukraine in 1924 and in Siberia in 1926.

51

"In the spring of 1923, Father sent Abram to Ekaterinov-ka to get some money for our emigration papers. Dad had written the petitions for us and the Driedigers (Sister Susan). They had been sent to Moscow for official approval. Now they had been returned, but Dad had no money to pay for them.

"Abe had to walk nearly seventy-five miles with little food to reach Susan's home. He walked for days and arrived total-ly exhausted. Sister Susan gave him supper and he fell asleep immediately. The next day he had to start the return jour-ney.

"Luckily, Jacob could sell his bull, which he had received as aid to his farm, for cash. Jacob gave the cash to Abram and he returned to us, under God's protection, with the needed money.

"Early in July of 1923, Father, Mother, Abram, Peter, George, Nick and I moved from No. 1 Nikolaipol to Ekateri-novka. Jacob Driediger came for us and helped us move. In Ekaterinovka he took us to the home of a widow whom we called Aunt Voat. Her daughter Anna lived with her. They gave us a place to stay until the crop could be harvested.

"As soon as the harvest was completed, Jacob and Dad drove the wheat to Chortitza to have it ground into flour. When they returned from selling their produce, we prepared for emigration. We baked buns and bread and started packing. In a few days, we received permission to leave.

"Jacob took us in his rack-wagon. Along with us was ano-ther person, and Jacob's cousin, Johann Rempel. Together we rode to No. 1 Nikolaipol eating our prepared breads and drinking water during our journey.

"We stayed in No. 1 Nikolaipol for two days and then drove to Chortitza. There was a freight train being loaded there with emigrants wanting to leave Russia. The last day, we and others were told that the train was full. What an agony. The Lord was looking after us though. In the after-noon one family decided not to go. Mr. Andreas, who was arranging the passengers, said, 'Well, Mr. Dyck, you are the next on the list.' Glory to God! We were delivered out of our misery.

Rack-wagon

"We rode the train to Riga, Latvia (now Latvian SSR). On the way we stopped at the Regiza station, on the line between Latvia and Russia, where medical checks were made and we had to disinfect (delouse) our clothes. Later, we boarded a boat and went through the Kiel Canal and finally arrived in Southampton, England. From there we went by train to Liverpool, England, where we boarded the *Montrosen*, for our trans-Atlantic trip. After we arrived in Quebec, Canada, we took the Canadian Pacific Railroad to Drake, Saskatchewan. We arrived in Drake on August 28, 1923. Here we were kindly welcomed.

"Father thanked God frequently for His blessing, guidance and leadership and he praised Him. Now we live here in Canada, each one in his own way. We want to accept God's blessings and not live indifferently, but praise and thank the Lord."

All migrations were not so happily ended. During the middle 1920s many thousands of Russians emigrated to Canada and the United States. Many others went to South American countries as quotas became filled. Often families were divided. These divisions always caused hardships.

An example of this in our family was the separation of my sister Susan and her husband Jacob. My sister and her two sons passed their physicals and were sent to Canada. Because of his eyes, Jacob was delayed for three months in England. By the time he was permitted to leave England, the Canadian quota was filled. Jacob went to Paraguay and after some time there, was allowed to rejoin his family in Canada. The Canadian government was lenient in this case. Some families remained separated.

In 1963 my brother Peter wrote to me informing me of this further example:

I want to tell you some news about H. B. from Kronsgarten, Russia. You or Sister Susan went to school with him. You should remember him. He married our cousin Marishen Wiens. He arrived here this year from Russia after spending many years in exile. He is now with his son H. in Saskatchewan, Canada. His wife, Marischen, died a long time ago in Paraguay, South America. His son

54

My Parents at home in Canada

Four Generations

H. moved here to Canada after the death of his mother. H. B. has a lot to tell of his experiences. Thank God that we are here in this country and all still alive.

My family, under the sponsorship of Jacob Wurz, went to live in Guernsey, Saskatchewan. Here my youngest half brother, Arthur, was born in 1926. The family moved to Harris, Saskatchewan in 1927 and farmed there until 1930. My in-laws, my growing family, and I visited them there in 1929 and enjoyed both a family reunion and the sights of a beautiful country.

My parents next bought a farm in Venn, Saskatchewan. They lived there until they moved to Yarrow, British Columbia, in 1941. In Yarrow they bought a strawberry farm. Dad was still farming in 1954 at the age of eighty-four.

Because of their advanced age, my parents finally had to live with my brother Abram and his family in Abbotsford, British Columbia. Though afflicted with frequent illness, my father, unable to remain idle for long, began riding his bicycle to town. This was commendable for a gentleman with such a record of suffering. He was still engaging in this exercise at the age of ninety-three.

My father, John John Dyck, passed away in an invalid hospital in Canada, in January, 1964. He was ninety-four years of age. At the time of his death Abram wrote:

> Yes, our dad sure had a long miserable life in the last years in Russia. He also had a lot of experience with God. He died believing in Jesus Christ our Lord and is with Him now. But *we* still have to fight until we pass too. Let's believe in Him to the end.

Chapter VI

LEAVING RUSSIA

My story resumes as the Republican Army, in the face of defeat, was retreating. General Wrangel, in charge of the Southern government, was trying to evacuate the White forces under his command from five ports in the Krym (Crimea). I was ordered to go to Yalta and from there, to leave the country.

I made my way south. As I went, I got what I could to eat and drink. I was drunk from eating over-ripe apples and drinking wine, but I remember reeling down the mountain and crossing the bridge into Yalta. I arrived only two hours before embarkation time and was ordered to get rid of my horse and get aboard ship.

My horse and I had been together for a long time. We had been a working team, sharing a common dependence upon one another. He had been my warmth against the cold, my transportation, and my companion. I had been his master and provider.

I led him away and tried to turn him loose. I smacked him and shooed him but he continued to follow me. I was running out of time. I had come too long a way to miss my ship because of a horse. General Wrangel was standing midship giving a speech when I pulled my revolver and shot my horse. This was a sad but necessary end to our partnership. Only then was I able to proceed to the ship.

There was standing room only on the coal freighter which was taking me away from war-torn Russia and life under the Communists. It was November, 1920 when I, along with 135,000 others on 126 boats left the country of our birth. This routing of men and ships from the southern coast marked the end of the Russian Civil War.

I was exhausted, both from my journey and from my

drunkenness. I needed sleep but there was a problem finding a place to lie down. As we left the port of Yalta, I took the fire hose out of its box, threw it into the sea, and slept in the box.

We were en route several days. All the ships went to Patrai, Greece. We stayed aboard ship there for a day and a half before continuing to Gallipoli, Turkey.

The French, at the end of World War I, had occupation troops in Turkey. While General Wrangel went to Paris to try to make a deal with the French to take our ships and supply us with food, all the men from our ships were held in a French concentration camp. This camp was like being held in a large bull pen. It had been hastily put together for our benefit. We were "protected" from the world by high walls and that was all. Our facilities were unroofed.

In the concentration camp we were helpless. We had no clothing, no money, and not enough food. I learned in a hurry to hate those who held me captive.

At Christmas time, we revolted. Forming a human chain, we escaped over the walls of that prison and proceeded to help ourselves. We took over a French supply freighter. We were a desperate lot and, considering the preceding years, men with little conscience; we were not hesitant about taking the things that we needed.

During the Revolution, I had received a decoration from the Republican army. While engaged in fighting near my home area, I had been sent through familiar territory to deliver a message. On my return, I came upon a White regiment trapped by a Communist force and unable to escape. Knowing every hill and ditch of the terrain, I was able, under the cover of night, to lead our troops to safety past the Bolsheviks. I was proud of my commendation, but past glory means little when your pockets are empty and your stomach is in a similar state. I traded my medal for a loaf of bread.

Arrangements for our displacement were finally made. Once again I boarded a freighter. This time we left Gallipoli, Turkey and proceeded to Istanbul (Constantinople) where we were under English supervision. Some of the men were sent to Batoum. George Lepp was the only one on board ship who could speak English. He took the names of all personnel.

In the town of Enikay, close to Istanbul, the American Mennonite Church had rented a house for the Russian Mennonite refugees. Here we waited until we could decide what to do. From here we made application for visas and awaited acceptance or rejection.

I have nothing but praise for the two organizations which helped my companions and me during our stay in Turkey. The first is the American Mennonite Church which provided a place for us to stay, and enabled us to borrow money. The other is the Salvation Army which provided us food and clothing without cost, when we so desperately needed it. Other organizations were there, but their help involved cost. To us, with no money, such help was no help at all.

A young man named Shraedes, and George Lepp contacted both the Netherlands and American consulates for visas for us. We were kept busy for a while getting our physical exams and other necessary papers. Then we waited, hoping some country would take us.

As luck would have it, I received a visa to go to the Netherlands. Two days later a visa to go to the United States arrived in my name. Which to accept caused me hours of weighing the pros and cons. I decided that I would go to the United States. I thought that perhaps all of Europe might be taken by the Communists, and I wanted to be as far away from them as possible.

A number of us embarked together from Istanbul for the United States. Among our group was John Wiebe, who settled in Orville, Ohio (Mr. Wiebe passed away May 7, 1966), Henry Penner, for whom I later worked in Massillon, Ohio, Abe Cape, Abe Dyck (no relation), Cornelius Berger, who settled in Massachusetts, and Abraham Hamm.

We didn't go directly to America. Our first ship stopped at Patrai, Greece. For several days we loaded cattle and grain on board. The ship also took on some Greek passengers. We delivered this load back to Turkey. Next we boarded a German-made Greek freighter named the *Alexandria*. From Turkey we went to Palermo, Sicily. Here we engaged in a few more days of loading—this time oranges and tangerines. Then

Declaration of Alien About to Depart for the United States

we left for America.

In all, it took about a year after leaving Russia to get to America. I was almost twenty-three years old when I was added to America's populace.

Chapter VII

A NEW LIFE

Early in 1922, I landed on Ellis Island in New York. Pete Zimmerly of Dalton, Ohio, had drawn my name and became my sponsor. He paid all my fares on ship and train from Istanbul to Dalton, Ohio.

In Dalton, I worked as a laborer in the Fisher Body Plant. The first English words I learned were cuss words which were shouted at me by the foreman. Such a vocabulary was not appropriate to my Mennonite upbringing nor was it acceptable to my new Mennonite friends, but the intonation of these new words was easy to understand.

I was anxious to improve myself. If I were going to live here, I wanted to fit in. I learned as much English as I could, as quickly as I could, and soon found myself foreman over the other Russian boys working in my section of the plant.

I was still staying with Pete Zimmerly when President Herbert Hoover went to Russia to set up a system of food distribution to help feed the starving Russian people. The Zimmerlys helped me gather clothes and food rations (World War I "K" rations) to send to my family still in Russia. Thanks to a number of Mennonite Church members in Sonnenberg, we collected nearly 400 pounds of clothing. We also had four boxes of food rations collected. Every month we sent more food. Once I sent money, which they never got.

Of the 400 pounds of clothing, my dad received only one shirt and a small pair of overalls. The rest was taken before it reached him. Dad had to sign that he had received the 400 pounds in order to receive even the shirt and overalls. This had been sent through the American Red Cross and a record was supposed to be kept. I confess I am still angry about this. I am sure that needy folk received the goods, but it was intended for those of my home and home area to whom I owed my allegiance.

I left the Fisher Body Plant after one year and went to Salem, Ohio. I took a job there with Mullens, learning automobile body finishing. Sometimes fenders were pretty thin when we finished filing them down to make them smooth, but I learned a lot and developed a skill. The training I received here would be invaluable to me. I remained in this work during my second year in America.

By April, 1923, I was able to repay my entire debt of $125.80 to the Mennonite Central Committee. This was the debt incurred during my wait for a visa in Constantinople.

I gave up factory work after a while and went with some other Russian boys, Henry Brown, John Wiebe, and George Lepp, to North Lima, Ohio. There we worked for different farmers in the community and could attend the local Mennonite church.

Many more Russian boys came to North Lima. I remember Henry Penner, Richard Kruegel, Abram Friesen, Peter Huebner, and two fellows named Derksen and Becker. There were also Dietrich Wheeler, Abram Cope, Abe Dyck, Cornelius Berger, Abraham Hamm and Jacob Huebert. Jacob Huebert led the singing at church.*

Strangely enough, Huebert and I came from the same area of Russia. His home was only twenty miles from my home in Kronsgarten. We knew each other in Russia and shared knowledge of the same people. I did not know that he had come to the United States and was greatly surprised to meet him again here. The group of boys who were together in North Lima have remained lifelong friends, keeping in contact these many years.

In 1924 and 1925 I worked for Ed Lehman, Sam Blosser and Melchior Mellinger. During this time I was tutored in English by Mr. Mellinger's older son, Clark, who was a high school teacher and I met Mr. Mellinger's older daughter, Ina. Ina was a talented girl. She should have finished school but she quit in her junior year of high school and began preparing for marriage. We were married in December of 1925 when Ina would have been a senior.

* See newspaper clipping concerning Huebert.

64

Cellist Who Served With White Russian Army Finds Life In Youngstown Is Good

Remembers Privations In Native Country As More Difficult Than Any Experienced In Depression

Jacob Huebert, first cellist with Youngstown's Little Symphony orchestra, has known worse depressions than the present one.

There are thousands of idle men in the Mahoning valley, but Mr. Huebert has seen millions idle.

"The people here in America do not know depression or hard times," he said. "I know, because I have existed thru them. I do not say 'lived', because 'existed' is the right word."

Mr. Huebert, a German, has known privation. He served with the Russian armies against the Germans in the World War.

Fought Bolsheviks

A Russian citizen, he fought in the White Army against the Russian Bolsheviks.

In those happy days before the World War he was one of a family of seven, living in Alexandrossk, Russia, where his German father had a brick yard.

They were prosperous folks and lived well. He went to the Russian "Gymnasium" in the town, graduating with what would be equivalent to a high school education here.

And he studied the cello in school and with the best masters in his community.

Nothing was too good for the boy, already rated something of a genius by men and women brought up with music from infancy and where every home had its own "artiste."

In Army At 21

At 21 he was in the Russian army, a German fighting against the Germans. He was on an ambulance train that brought the wounded from the front into Moscow.

A year later he was enrolled in the White Army fighting for the czar against the Bolsheviks. He served there two years and was one of 150,000 refugees who escaped by ship to Constantinople in 1920.

There, under the guardianship of the American relief agencies, he lived for eight months, waiting his opportunity to come to America, Canada, anywhere, where he could make a living.

Early in 1921 he docked in New York, one of several thousand refugees looking only for the opportunity to make enough to eat and sleep. He did not speak a word of English. He did not have a cent of

Jacob Huebert, Little Symphony Cellist

Fingers Now Sensitive To Touch Of Instrument Once Were Stiffened By Hard Work On Farms

it. But he was urged and so that night he played Golterman's "The Dream", and Tschaikowsky's wailing "Chanson Triste". An ovation greeted him.

Studied With Hensel

Encouraged, he came to Youngstown and resumed his studies under the direction of Henry Hen-

money. He had been separated from his family, located later in Canada.

Went To Columbiana

The American Relief agencies got him a job as a farmhand with Elmer Shank of Columbiana and there he arrived to find friendly folks ready to share with him a comfortable home and happy surroundings.

For four years he worked on the farm, doing the regular work of a farm hand.

His hands became rough and his fingers lost their elasticity. He believed that he would never play again, but always he kept in mind the training of his boyhood and the family hope that he would be a musician.

In October of 1926 they were getting up an entertainment at the Reformed church at North Lima. The farm hand was asked to play the cello. He did not think he could do

sel, a cellist with the Cleveland Symphony orchestra.

Carmine Ficocelli had been engaged to have a stringed quartet play for the Duca del Abruzzi banquet at the Italian hall. He could not locate a cellist and Mr. Reardon advised him to have Mr. Huebert.

"He played beautifully," says Mr. Ficocelli. "He played the way men play only when they love and understand their instrument and the technique and mastering of it."

Lived In Columbiana

Six months ago he married Grace Lehman of North Lima, one of the members of that audience who heard the farm hand try his luck at the concert back in 1926. They live at 571 W. LaClede.

When the Little Symphony stages the second in its series of concerts here Feb. 9 at South high school, the solo cello parts will be played by Mr. Huebert.

Many things were against a successful marriage for us. Ina was seventeen while I was an old man of twenty-six. I was an immigrant with broken English, no money, and not many connections, but we were young and full of hope. We knew we would have to work hard, but we wanted to share our lives.

It was not strange in those times to begin a marriage living with the family. We lived in the south end of the Mellinger family home, which was a nine-room farmhouse often used for two families. Our first child, Ena, was born at home in 1927.

In 1928 I made an application for U. S. citizenship. On June 7, in Youngstown, Ohio, I became a naturalized citizen. I hold certificate No. 2764450. On this certificate I officially had my name corrected from John Dick to John Dyck.

Ina's second brother, Port, was in the nursery business with her father. Dad Mellinger and Port had bought a house which adjoined the farm. In 1928 our little family moved into this house, which had formerly been a schoolhouse. Port and his new bride moved into the family home with his parents and younger sister, Essie. Our new home was very pleasant. It had been nicely remodeled and was surrounded by huge maple trees. Our next two children, John John, Jr. and Anton, were born in this, our second home.

I worked for Dad Mellinger and Port on the farm for the first five and a half years of my marriage to Ina. For my work we received the use of the house, our vegetables and other farm produce, plus some money. Toward the end of this period, America entered the depression years and this arrangement became too difficult for all of us to continue. There simply was not enough income to maintain us all.

It was April of 1931 when Ina and I gathered our three children, Ena, almost four, John Jr., two years old, and Anton, ten months old, climbed into our old car and left Ohio. We had decided to try pioneering in Canada.

Ina looked on our pioneering days as a storybook adventure. She was as wide-eyed and excited as a child when we began and, to the end, was confident that we would be able to succeed in our venture. She dedicated herself, body and

66

heart, to prove that our "doubting Thomas" friends and relations were wrong, and that we were stronger than the elements and the times.

After our arrival in Venn, Saskatchewan, we stayed for the first six months with my parents while we looked for a farm to buy. Without land of our own to plant, I worked for my dad and for other neighboring farmers that first summer in Canada. Ina helped with the chores at home. In this way we earned our keep and our supplies for the long cold winter ahead.

In September of 1931 we found the farm we had been looking for. It was near the small town of Watrous, Saskatchewan, not far from my parents' home. Here in our tight little one-room cabin we were at last able to be alone as a family.

Our land fronted on the edge of Lake Manitou. Around us were blue hills, bush, and prairie country. We were lacking in material things, but we did possess the satisfaction of our independence and the beauties and wonders of the country. No wealth could replace rainbows at night, the fantasy of the northern lights, the wildlife, and the vastness of the land.

Ina and I applied for a loan to buy our farm. The cost was $500 with $100 down and $100 a year for four years. We were to pay six percent interest.

Life was a continuous struggle. We worked from sunup to long after sundown, building and remodeling our cabin and trying to make a living from the land. Our nearest neighbors were three miles away. Transportation in winter was horseback or wagon, facing temperatures of 40 and 50 degrees below zero.

Ina began giving piano lessons for fifty cents a lesson and earned cash, livestock, and supplies for her efforts. She rode horseback, eventually covering a twenty-mile circuit, to reach her students. Sometimes she had to stay overnight at the homes of her pupils when the elements provided too much mud or snow to allow her to complete her journey.

In Canada my young children brought back to me the things I had done in my early childhood. It was there that they received some of the blisterings which they will recall to

67

their old ages. They set fire to a wheat field, let the cows into the corn field, and played hooky from school. They also added to the daily dilemma by having all the childhood diseases one right after another.

Because of my not being a Canadian citizen, very few jobs were open to me. I could hire myself out for farm labor, which I did, but this caused me to be away from home a great deal—sometimes for a month at a time. I did not like leaving Ina alone with the children and all the chores to look after, but if we were to have supplies, it was necessary.

We planted our vegetable garden in the spring and tended cows, pigs, and chickens. In the fall we gathered wild berries and fruits and were able to provide pretty well for our needs. There were always staples such as sugar, flour and clothes for which we needed cash. Remaining always in the back of our minds was the need to hoard the tax and loan money.

Each succeeding year we were only able to pay the interest on our loan. We tried to earn more money by producing vegetables not commonly grown. Some of our seed sent from Ohio grew well in the soil. Some did not. In 1935 we had an exceptional potato year—but so did everyone else. One summer, peas were hard to get. We had a good crop so we received a good price for these. Sometimes eggs were high, but at other times it only paid to eat them ourselves. Such are the chances a farmer takes.

In the summers I began taking garden vegetables daily to the lake resort nearby. Here I could get a good price for the fresh produce from the people vacationing there. Things were looking up. During the winter months I cut and corded the lumber on our land and sold it. Ina remade clothes sent by her family and made do with the few material possessions we had.

Whether things were up or down, there were always friends and family dropping in. This was the way of life. Everyone came, stayed, and ate. This was hospitality and when things were going well, it was fine. There were many times though when there was little food for our own family, but company still came and ate.

Here in the bush we found that people were there, ready

Ina with our children
Anton, John, and Ena in Canada

to help you or your neighbor, when trouble came. If you had anything extra, you took it to someone who was without. When they had something they could help you with, they did. We were people bound together sharing our common problems.

1936 brought us another baby, Clark. Ina's health had not been good, but the baby was healthy and Ina regained her strength after a time. Our debts had been growing so we were forced to sell our car. Hope for a better "next year" was still strong within us.

The spring of 1937 was beautiful. All the settlers set about planting a large crop and working the soil. The beautiful promise was not to be ours, however. Summer brought 114° heat and no rain. As rainless weeks limped into months, wells dried up. There was no harvest. Any vegetation which was left, the grasshoppers and army worms took. Feed for stock was very scarce for the coming winter. The cattle were sold or sent to other areas for wintering. Farmers were cutting Russian thistle for winter feed for remaining stock.

Drought hit everyone in Saskatchewan, Alberta and Manitoba. We were lucky because we only had to haul water for the house one mile, while some people had to go twenty miles to supply their water need. We had watered our strawberries as long as we could, but we got no berries. There weren't even any wild ones. Of the winter vegetables, only potatoes were harvested.

I thought of going to Idaho to find work. The family would remain on the farm. Instead, we decided to return to Ohio where I could find work in the auto body field.

I preceded the family to Massillon, Ohio. I found employment and a place to live before sending for the family. We spent a year in Massillon in not-too-fine circumstances living as unaccustomed city folk.

I had a job offer from my old friend Paul Gilmore in auto body work in Wooster, Ohio, and jumped at the opportunity. We moved to Creston, Ohio, a small, rural community nearby. Here we lived in the area of town people used to call "Hell's half acre," but it was much nicer than the crowded city and still near my job. We were near open fields, woods,

Dorothy and I with our children:
Philip, Anton, Shirley and Clark

Three Generations of John Dycks

71

and muck areas. We could stretch, breathe, and grow here. We could garden in rich muck land and raise our own vegetables. We soon learned to love this friendly community.

Ina continued to help the family financially. In our home she ran a kind of kindergarten nursery school. She also had a club called "Torch Bearers" after school for somewhat older children. She also wrote poetry, and succeeded in having some of her work accepted by magazines.

For some time after coming back to the States, we continued to hold on to the hope of owning our lake farm in Canada. To do this we would have to scrape up five dollars a month. We still owed $455 of the original $500 after eight years. Finally, we had to abandon this dream.

Ina and I moved our family to our second Creston home on Burbank Street after our fifth child, Philip, was born in 1941. Ina developed pancreatitis and died of complications following surgery. Her passing left a great void in our lives. This was 1943.

I married Dorothy Double Keltz in 1945. She had been a kind friend and neighbor since we had come to Creston. She helped Ina with our home and children during Ina's illnesses and continued to help manage my household after Ina's death. Dot brought to our marriage two children, Bill and Shirley, and made our family complete with seven children.

When Paul Gilmore went out of business, I was in a position to buy some of his equipment and try business on my own. I would not be happy until I tried it.

I opened my own body and fender shop on Salt Street in Rittman, Ohio. I was particular about my workmanship and I could offer my customers quality work, with the additional attraction of a lower price.

With seven healthy, growing eaters in the family and with my business fluctuating with the times, our income was sometimes inadequate. When a man needs help, it is gratifying to find it forthcoming from his family. Dorothy and the older children pitched in and worked outside our home to aid our finances. This combined effort gave us a modest but comfortable living with the necessities provided. We have been rich in our happiness together.

72

Four Russian friends together again

My first grandchild

Granddaughter Beth and I
visiting in California, 1964

A good car needs a good polish

I love to see things grow

Working in the Tastee Freez

In the mid 1950s, Dot and I, along with Naomi and Jay Lance, (her sister and brother-in-law), decided to try running a business together. We applied for and were given the franchise to operate a new Tastee Freez ice cream parlor which was built on the edge of town.

Dot and Naomi manned the business during the day and every second evening. Jay and I continued in our regular work during the day and were ice cream salesmen on the odd nights.

Until I got involved with the ice cream business, I did not know how much work it would be. It was sticky, messy, and heavy. Preparing food for the public involved a lot of back-breaking work. After preparing and serving it, we still had the never-ending job of cleaning.

This was no work for us to do. After working all day, serving part of the night, stocking and cleaning, we were worn out. We managed to make it through two years but gave it up for a less hectic life.

Through the years, I built up my automobile body and fender business clientele until I was able to move to a better location in Rittman. I ran a one-man business. On occasion I tried to employ helpers for some of the work, but the quality of their work did not please me. I continued in this work until my retirement.

My health forced me into retirement in 1959. Since then, I have taken it easy, like a penniless millionaire. The children are all grown and away from home. Dorothy continued to work as a salesclerk at Freedanders (a nice department store) in Wooster, Ohio. When the cold of the Ohio winter became intolerable for me, I vacillated between my desire to live in a warmer climate, leaving a place where we were at home, and had acquired friends and possessions, and staying where winter turns home into a prison for me, but where family is near and other seasons are beautiful.

Finally the decision was made. In 1964 we sold our home. Dorothy and I, with the combined talents of my sons, John, Jr., Philip and my son-in-law William Taylor, built our new home just outside of Creston. In this new home I could work in my garden, enjoy my family, and putter around the house.

A proud father poses with his son, Clark,
after graduation from U.S. Naval Academy

I have been blessed in my life. The Lord has seen fit to give me two life partners, warm, hard working and dear. He blessed me with fine, healthy children eager to pursue their own destinies. He guided me to this country which has been good to me and which has left me free to make my life as rich as my abilities would allow. For what more can a man ask?

* * * * *

John John Dyck, Sr. passed from this life June 4, 1966 following a heart attack. He had had a number of attacks since 1959. Welding and painting, through the years, finally took their toll. He lived the last seven of his years enjoying the additional time which he was granted and making his peace with his Lord. During this time, he visited his family in Canada and his son in California, where this narrative was started. He kept himself available to his children. His wife, Dorothy, was a comfort and help to him to the end.

S. M.D.

When Miss Liberty extends her invitation to the world's "tired and poor," she does not usually roll out a red carpet for those she receives. Perhaps she is a wise benefactress. She provides those who adopt her with the opportunity to prove their own worth.

We built a new home

Agatha Dyck Langemann